David Gentleman's INDIA

A John Curtis Book
Hodder & Stoughton
LONDON SYDNEY AUCKLAND

For Fenella

© 1994 by David Gentleman

First published in 1994
by Hodder and Stoughton
A division of Hodder Headline PLC
Trade paperback 1995

The right of David Gentleman to be identified as the author of
this work has been asserted by him in accordance with the
Copyright, Designs and Patents Act 1988.

10 9 8 7 6 5 4 3 2 1

British Library Cataloguing in Publication Data
A catalogue record for this book
is available from the British Library

ISBN 0 340 61740 3

Photoset by Rowland Phototypesetting Ltd,
Bury St Edmunds, Suffolk

Printed and bound in Italy by L.E.G.O., Vicenza

Hodder and Stoughton Ltd
A Division of Hodder Headline PLC
338 Euston Road
London NW1 3BH

Contents

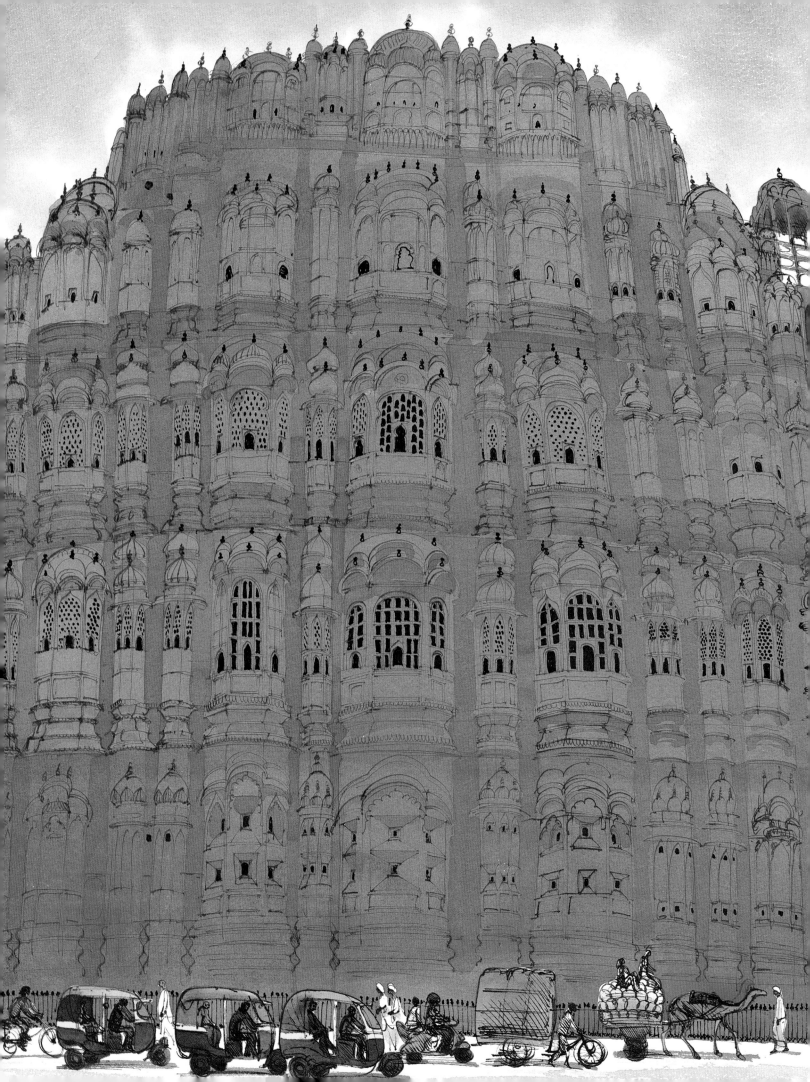

Introduction

The name 'India' is misleading. It suggests somewhere precise and finite; like, say, Spain. But India is not a definite, hard-edged and self-contained country. It is a diverse place, made up of many different states with different histories, cultures, languages, landscapes, costumes and people. An hour or two's flight can take one into extraordinary extremes not only of different ways of life but of climate, from snowy mountain and arid desert to tropical forest. And its various areas seem often to belong to different centuries. Bombay is a westernised modern skyscraper city; Jaisalmer seems almost medieval, its winding streets full of shoemakers, goatherds, millers, tailors, weavers, scribes, stone-breakers, saddlers and masons: all the familiar characters from a traditional fairy story, people who have long vanished from the European scene.

How then can one begin to give any impression of such a large and bewildering subject as the Indian subcontinent, with all its people and spectacle? In order to convey its enormous geographical and human diversity, its delights and curiosities, one has to pick out some of the things that are most typical of each region, and to identify also the many features that are found nowhere else; things that, wherever you are, give the unmistakable flavour and character of Indian life, the clear and vivid certainty of being in India. To this end, I made three extended journeys in India in 1992 and 1993, covering the country from top to bottom and from side to side, and drawing all the time.

The Indian countryside often looks just as one hoped it would. Here are the creaking bullock carts, the big camels, the elephants, the teams of oxen panting and snorting as they plough; the brown mud huts and the light thatched dwellings which seem hardly more substantial than stacks of crops; the thin, wiry peasant women carrying backbreaking bundles of firewood or water pots or heaps of fodder on their heads. Here are the paddyfields with water gleaming among the shoots of rice, and white egrets wading in them, and the rich fields of familiar wheat and barley or unfamiliar cotton, sugarcane, or millet; and here are wells and dried-up rivers, craggy hills topped by fierce-looking fortresses, roads shaded by tunnels of great banyans with creepers hanging from them. The work in the fields is traditional, timeless, biblical, labour-intensive; especially beautiful at harvest time when the cut fields are full of neat rows of hand-tied sheaves, as if in a landscape by Stubbs, creating an impression of benign and necessary husbandry. The chaff is still winnowed by hand from the grain at the edge of the harvest field; bullocks are gently washed down in the stream; tired peasants in white or coloured cotton clothes return to their villages at the end of the day. But in the richer areas, there are plenty of new machines too: combine harvesters and big tractors, garlanded just as the bullocks' horns are painted and their sides stencilled with coloured patterns. The old, unmechanised farming methods must have been workable and durable for the land to have survived; will it last so long under mechanisation, and with so many more millions to feed?

Hawa Mahal, Jaipur

So the country is lovely. But country and town may be hard to separate. In many beautiful places in India a civilisation has flourished and then been reclaimed by the countryside. Mandu and Bijapur too were once extraordinary centres of civilisation, their complex and perfect buildings remaining but surrounded now by small, insignificant towns that are hardly more than villages. The climate has been kind to the old buildings: time has not cracked or crumbled their stones. Hampi's bazaars and temples have not been submerged beneath later development but simply left standing, neglected but unharmed, as a backdrop to wandering cattle and groups of children. They are surrounded not by suburbia but by an enchanting landscape of tall sugarcane and banana plantations, watered by a great winding river, the stones strewn at its bank embellished here and there with skilfully carved figures which, amid so much other fine workmanship, no one even notices. Wherever one looks the hills are covered with big boulders, some of them broken open where sections have been split off to be used for building. From a hilltop vantage point one sees the relics of a magnificent city, with avenues, temples and long lines of small shop units, empty now or with families camping out in them. One can no longer imagine such tranquil and abandoned isolation in Europe.

There are good things everywhere in the Indian countryside: the beauty and fascination of the people, the strangeness of the sounds and smells, the curiosity and unfamiliarity of the buildings. But in the bigger towns and cities, wonders and horrors are mixed up together: not so much the smug and patronising western clichés of disease and starvation but the hellish glimpses of discomfort and squalor on pavements and in shanty towns, made worse by the contrast with surrounding prosperity and by noisy dense traffic. And yet I was told that the pavement people feel lucky to have escaped from village life.

All the same, it was just this confused and endless pattern of ordinary daily life that I found most intriguing to draw: buses and lorries and autorickshaws, laden animals and equally laden people, rich and poor, beautifully and picturesquely clothed; the cattle all mixed up amongst the traffic and yet surviving, whereas in a western city the only cows you see are in bits, at the butcher's.

Agra

In drawing such things, and describing them, a certain detachment may help. But it is hard to be objective. I can't look at the sexy sculptures of Khajuraho or Konarak, Badami or Hampi, without wondering what their purpose was, what was in the minds of their remarkable sculptors. And I can't look at an Indian landscape or town without thinking about how the people in them exist, about living conditions, and caste; or without reflecting on the harm so obviously being done to forests and to the land by the present rampaging modernisation of all India. Market forces had nothing to do with the creation of any of the things one goes to India to see; but faith in these unreliable forces, in consumerism, is replacing the equilibrium of the past, with its carved and garlanded bulls and its gods riding on the backs of peacocks.

Badami

Travelling in India is fun: getting up at four in the morning to board a plane at dawn; riding on an ancient train – maybe in the engine – or on elephants or camels, or in bumpy autorickshaws; meeting people with unexpected lifestyles and opinions; clambering about ruins or up rocky hills; buying 'safe' fruit like bananas and oranges from hawkers or off barrows, or slaking one's thirst with fresh lime sodas or cold beer; sleeping in bare and modest rest-houses under a mosquito net or – quite inexpensively – in a rajah's palace.

But India is vast, and getting about it is complicated. Many of its most interesting places are remote, involving a flight or a very long railway journey followed by a further trip by bus or car. Agra, where a fast train from Delhi deposits you at the very gate of the fort, is an exception. But the long train journeys are worth it: you are surrounded by many strata of Indian society, not only by the rich who can afford to fly; it is a good way to see the landscape and the people in it, and to make the kind of friends that if one is new to the place or timid may at first seem alarming. A car with a driver costs less than hiring a car and driving it

Varanasi

yourself does in Europe. My various drivers were tireless and nice, and patient about my stops to draw or take photographs. Sometimes I hired guides; almost all were interesting, pleasant and well-informed, and could always tell me far more than I could possibly take in.

Looking at India is interesting and demanding – getting to places, forming an impression of them and trying to understand them needs energy and staying-power. Doing this on one's own is lonely, but when alone one is more exposed to others and more receptive to impressions of places and ways of life, and to other visitors, Indian and European. But when travelling alone, one's moods swing more wildly than at home, from fascination and elation to exhaustion, panic and despair – even on occasion almost to regret at ever having come at all. At first I was taken aback by these changing spirits; but after I noticed that they followed a pattern – enthusiasm in the morning, despair only when I felt worn out – it was easy to keep them in proportion.

One disturbing aspect of India is that, to be there for any length of time, one must be much richer than most of the people one meets. This makes one feel guilty, but it's inescapable: if it were not so, one wouldn't be there at all. And being there entails other shocks – more so than anywhere else I know. One catches alternating glimpses of paradise and inferno; life looks briefer, tougher and dodgier than it does at home. There is the additional surprise of coming across strange customs, which even the unlikeliest people still subscribe to. And there are the occasional minor frustrations when simple acts – buying a ticket, posting a parcel, going to the bank – become lengthy, tedious and frustrating adventures. My travels were also disrupted from time to time by strikes, riots and curfews, but nothing went seriously wrong.

India is now much more expensive than when I first went there in the sixties. Even so, European travellers are still privileged and protected by their wealth; even poorish students have more to spend than most Indians; if need be, one can take refuge in a comfortable hotel, safely cocooned and sealed off from Indian realities as if in a space-ship, able in the last resort, if the experience becomes too much for one, to escape – to Nepal or Thailand, or simply back home. But escape is the option most Indians do not have.

Indian weather is predictable – surprisingly so to Europeans – with unvaryingly clear skies, but usually without the interest (for an artist) of clouds, their lovely shapes and perspectives and moving shadows; often there is nothing to draw in the sky. Because of the latitude, the sun rises and falls quickly and almost vertically: dawns and sunsets are very beautiful, but quickly over. Days are short – the length of spring or autumn days in Europe. Stars are bright and clear but our familiar constellations have vanished to the north. A half-moon appears, not vertical, on its side as in Britain, but horizontal, like a half-grapefruit on a plate, or – towards morning – like an igloo. The seasons are not so clearly differentiated as ours are.

Mowgli would be lonely today. While I was in India, apart from squirrels, bats and monkeys, I saw almost no wild animals: a mongoose by the roadside once, a dead snake, a few wild pigs in a game reserve. All the camels and elephants I saw were domesticated. But there are many beautiful birds, usually much tamer than in Europe: groups of noisy green parrots, always in a hurry; crested hoopoes, bulbuls, paddy-birds, birds whose tail-feathers curl at the ends, a strange mad-sounding bird with a cackle like dotty laughter, and vultures and kites, magnificent in flight. And sometimes at dusk the sky will fill with enormous bats, flapping slowly and unsteadily as they circle in the crowded air before they all head off in the same direction for the night's feeding.

When drawing, one notices sounds very acutely – wind, birds, leaves. But most Indian sounds are human: early morning Hindu puja (prayers) or the Muslim muezzin; hawking and spitting as people begin the day; the patient, monotonous swish-swish of the sweeper's light broom; the steady slapping noise of washing being beaten on a stone; music, drumming and firecrackers.

But the most pervasive human sound of all is speech; and the speech that you attend to is English. Indian English has its own rhythms and timbre and usages: one is 'charred' to death, not merely 'burnt'; one's job is one's 'duty', which gives doing it a strongly pious ring. Children's questions are direct: 'Hello, Mr Painter-man! What is your good name? From which place?' English is still the usual language for anything that really needs to be understood: instructions, traffic signs, newspapers and advertisements.

Jodhpur

In India certain realities of life appear straight and unvarnished. Physique, emotion, hardship, deprivation, even death – things often masked or hidden in Europe – appear as they really are. Even facial expressions seem natural and frank rather than reserved – people don't 'put a good face' on things in India. And although people seem dressed for modesty rather than display, the warm climate and the light clothing reveal them truly, as they really are: graceful or bent, beautiful or ugly, there is little pretence. Indian clothes reveal touchingly vulnerable parts of the body – the midriff and the small of a back under a saree, a thigh in a dhoti, calves under shorts or a lunghi, feet and toes in sandals or barefoot. Light cotton clothes also suggest the underlying structure of the body: strong sinewy shoulders, the inward curve of the back, broad hips, divided buttocks, springy thighs, lithe and muscular physique or folds of unused flesh. Physical labour makes bodies look spare and graceful and fully used: they seem not titillatingly erotic but real and true.

Orchha

But harsher aspects are revealed too: powerful, bullying faces, or broken ones; tough and cruel-looking police and soldiers; the frail and helpless, not tucked away out of sight as they are in Europe; beggars, their plight marketed and commercialised. For many people, work begins early in life, and they look worn-out much sooner than Europeans do. And one is aware of the quick turn-over of generations, and of the presence of death – not kept discreetly out of sight but going up in flames conspicuously and for all to see.

I enjoyed and was spurred on by the examples of three earlier artist-writers who had kept journals and drawn in India. The first and best-connected was Fanny Eden, sister of the Governor-General of India, a better writer than her more famous sister Emily and a vivid draughtswoman. The others were both professionals: Edward Lear and Edward Ardizzone. Lear's *Indian Journal* of 1874–6 is clear and honest as he both enjoys and deplores what he has let himself in for. Ardizzone's *Indian Diary* of 1952–3 is short and pithy. Both journals of course have marvellous drawings.

Drawing in the street in India is not easy. It's hot and dry and dusty: sometimes one feels that one may be inhaling trouble with every breath. One needs a patch of shade, for comfort and to stop the ink drying on the pen; and plenty of bottled drinking water, which luckily is in good supply. I soon got used to the feeling of sweat trickling down inside my shirt, front and back, like a stream of ants. But working this way has its rewards. If you want peace, you can usually find an inconspicuous or inaccessible place where you aren't disturbed. On the street, people are friendly and curious about the process of drawing, and have time on their hands; they become protective, shooing newcomers out of one's line of vision; they are disarmingly and disconcertingly frank. A soft-drinks seller told me he was getting married the next month, an arranged match. 'Oh good! To someone nice?' – 'No' . . . (Pause) . . . 'But *quite* nice.'

If the people standing in front of me blot out the view entirely, I can always draw them instead. And since drawing, here as elsewhere, is now an unusual thing to be doing, people are curious about it, and the normal roles – tourist as onlooker, Indian as reluctant object of curiosity – are reversed: the artist is the one who gets stared at and briefly provides the interest. This seems a fair exchange. Drawing people seems generally to be thought of as a friendly activity, whereas photographing them is often resented, as if something is being taken away – which in a way it is.

But when gathering information against the clock, a camera is useful. I used to take photographs carefully and deliberately, but drawing leaves no energy to spare for this; instead, my camera has become a copying machine, a notebook, and I photograph whatever I've drawn as a sort of check or reminder. A camera is quick and neutral; you need a great many photographs to tell you as much as you can see by simply looking at something, but you can also photograph far more things than there would ever be time to draw. For this very reason, because it is so quick and easy to use, one can be tempted to grab too much information, take too many pictures, in order to avoid missing something interesting or having to come back another day; whereas, when drawing, one has to be more careful about choosing a subject because one is committing more time and energy to it, and the selection – the thinking – has to be done before the pen touches the paper.

I tried to draw India objectively, without preconceptions, and without grinding any axes. But it isn't easy to look at the changing scene with complete detachment, because how it looks makes one ask why it is that way. Drawing allows one to stare, to be curious, to watch closely without seeming inquisitive. And it gives one a chance to watch the oddities of the passing scene at length: an old car body being trundled laboriously along the street on a barrow, a fleet of donkeys carrying bags of bricks, a fist fight between fishermen over their catch.

Manmad

But once the matter of what to draw struck me sharply and uncomfortably. It was during the Ayodhya riots, on a railway platform, as I waited for the Goa–Delhi train. Underneath a painted notice saying 'Ticketless travel is a social evil' a striking and fine-looking old man, wrapped in blankets, sat on the platform. I drew him as unobtrusively as I could, and asked someone if he was a saddhu or holy man? – 'No – just an economically disadvantaged'. As I went on drawing, surrounded now by porters and other good-natured onlookers, a bossy official came up and asked, 'Why are you drawing this scheduled (i.e. untouchable) person? You should be drawing Indian landscapes to show your friends at home, not people like this. From whom did you take permission?' I began to get cross and said I'd never in my life sought such permission; adding rather pompously that the truth was always valuable in itself, and sufficient justification. He said, by now enraged, 'You have no right to take such images of India and to give foreigners a wrong impression. I am a security official: I *forbid* you to draw this man.' I wouldn't stop drawing, said he was a fool, and that he'd better get a policeman to back him up. One was instantly found, but he was too embarrassed or overwhelmed to do anything; and eventually the security man blustered off, leaving me alone to bask in the approval of the porters until a pleasant, serious-looking man who had been watching the encounter said, 'All right – you've made your point and I agree with you. But a lot of people have died in this country over these last few days, and this is a bad time for anyone to find himself at the centre of a noisy crowd, whatever the reason. You'd do better to sit quietly in the waiting room and read a book until the train comes.' And this I did; reflecting as my anger cooled that what seemed to me interesting and worth recording might indeed hurt someone else's pride or sense of honour, and even make them justifiably angry.

To anyone brought up on European architecture and used to drawing it, Indian buildings at first look fascinating but perplexing. The Mughal monuments – the Delhi tombs, the Taj Mahal, Bijapur – are made up of familiar enough elements – cubes, cylinders, hemispheres – though their arches and domes are tantalisingly subtle in form. But the great Hindu temples are in a new and altogether confusing architectural language, in which one can take nothing for granted: everything needs to be looked at individually, bit by bit. There are no regular patterns, no helpful divisions into bays made up of repeated units, no familiar and reassuring repetition; everything is strange and intricate in its detail. And much is encrusted with inventive and unfamiliar pattern, or covered with figures, realistic or grotesque, of people or animals or imaginary beings, many of them malevolent, who you have to learn to identify.

Apart from the Mughals and the British, whose works are easy to recognise, in general I could not easily keep track of which successive layer of the past, which temporary civilisation or occupying power, had been responsible for which historic site. But however puzzling and complicated they may look, I loved the beauty and the subtlety of the old rock temples, in which carved figures and decoration are inseparable from the structure which in turn is itself indistinguishable from – part of – the surrounding rock. When the Parthenon was built its sculptures were simply placed in position – added and easily removable. But in the cave temples everything has been cut or carved from the single solid rock – easy to deface but impossible to remove.

Badami

Ooty

There is another inescapable architectural style, more familiar to European eyes and yet unique to India. This is the solid and almost indestructible building style of the Raj: seen not only in its great set-pieces like the Victorian splendours of Bombay, but in many lesser military and administrative buildings and rest-houses, with their grandly arched portals and their imposing gateways onto the road: solid and complacent and rather ugly buildings which have remained in use or survived neglect, almost unscathed.

On a grander scale are the splendid eighteenth- and nineteenth-century remains in Calcutta, the old capital city of the Raj, and in Madras and Bombay: places built to house the institutions of law and learning, government and the church; and the great railway stations, monuments to a unified and manageable country, that held India together in a practical way. And then, from this century and in a class of their own, are the astonishing New Delhi buildings of Baker and Lutyens, the first capable and skilful, the second brilliant and inspired; men at odds with each other who nevertheless between them gave a compelling form to the rhetoric of Empire, just as it was becoming clear that the whole thing was done for.

Another Raj idiom, less overbearing and often rather touching, is the one that was meant to remind the British of 'home': used for telegraph offices and post offices, picturesquely transplanted Gothic churches, libraries and small houses, often of wood and with corrugated-iron roofs and fretted verandahs, cast-iron railings and nostalgic or sentimental English names – the kind of buildings that linger on, precariously unloved and neglected, in the former hill stations of Shiimla and Darjeeling, Mount Abu and Ooty.

Coming from Britain, I could never escape at least the reminders of the time when the British held immense sway in India, and an uneasy sense of Britain's past involvement – 'divide and rule' – in its subsequent disintegration into ill-adjusted communities. Attitudes and tensions from this period, even though diluted by time, still colour the relationships: however one might wish to, it's impossible not to be reminded of the Raj – not as a romantic and picturesque institution, the jewel in the imperial crown, which it clearly was, but as an unfair, harsh and eventually unsustainable imposition. In any case, there are in North Delhi too many half-blown-up buildings, fortifications, memorials and other reminders of the Mutiny or the first war of Independence for one to be able to forget it, even if one wanted to.

Religion with all its rituals and preoccupations is as pervasive, as inescapable in India as the climate: intriguing, mysterious, strident or irritating; sometimes touching, sometimes consisting of mere din, sometimes dangerous or even deadly, as I realised when, after being holed up in a hotel during the Ayodhya rioting, I eventually emerged to find the streets full of glass and the buses and trains with broken windows. Religion is also noisy: in a holy place like Pushkar religion wakens one at five in the morning with prolonged and amplified Brahmin chanting; Jains ping temple bells: Goan Christians bang drums, blow trumpets and let off thunderflashes before and during Mass. And religion crops up in odd places: one morning inside a bank I saw the armed security guard, rifle over his shoulder, doing puja (worship) at a small shrine by the manager's office; one sees brightly coloured shrines by the roadside, in people's houses, in deserted places or on city streets; a driver will stop in the middle of the countryside to pay respect to the roadside shrine of the same god whose tiny plastic image dangles and lights up above his dashboard. And in temples and shrines and on packets of sliced bread, one sees and soon recognises the Hindu gods and their accoutrements: elephant-headed Ganesh, monkey-faced Hanuman, many-armed Siva, furious-looking Durga and so on. To begin with, these creatures look freakish: curious but unappealing inventions, Wellsian or Disneyish mutants, as significant as two-headed chickens. But quite soon I grew simply to accept them as odd but familiar, and to take pleasure in recognising them. Visiting a temple is less confusing when you know who the carved figures represent: it is like having a smattering of a language.

Dewas

Some people go to India in search of a spiritual experience of some sort – understanding, enlightenment or peace of mind. These would be benefits worth having; but I didn't seek, or find, any such experiences. Although the Indian temples and mosques are fascinating architecturally and their paintings and carvings are beautiful and moving, everyday Indian religious practices seemed on balance unattractive, at worst repellent. One might have hoped that some kind of Indian calm, resignation or philosophical acceptance of the inevitable might have rubbed off on one: more likely perhaps when one is away from home and normal routine. But it didn't. And even if a long spell in India might have made European life seem needlessly feverish and ambitious, this is just how Indian life now seems too. All the same, visiting India impels one to reconsider one's own life: to think of it as measured in other ways than by the accumulation of things, achievements, jobs done; and to reflect that European goals and assumptions, even those the Indians are adopting most eagerly, may be illusory.

What I did sense was fascination with the strange realities of India, and a confirmation of what should already have been clear enough: that experience of people, landscape, the life around one, is the only reality; and that the time one has for this is short. This is worth remembering; but one needn't go to India to work it out.

The distant past continues in India. Either because it was indestructible, like the ancient Ashokan pillars, or inaccessible, as at Hampi, or forgotten, as at Ajanta, or still in daily operation, as in the southern temples, it has survived; and, except in the cities, it has escaped being blotted out by the present. And many ordinary things in India seem strange, foreign, exotic and yet half-familiar – as if they belong to a past that we have now outgrown and discarded. The Indian countryside reminds us of our own European past, because there our old ways still survive.

But across the fields, beyond the palaces and forts, one sees the tall chimney of a chemical works or a power station, a satellite dish or a red and white striped radio mast; and the streets of even the smallest villages are now an intricate maelstrom not only of people, cattle, carts and bicycles but of tractors, lorries, buses and motor scooters. Dress is changing too – more people now wear practical western clothes – jeans and tee-shirts instead of lunghis, dhotis, pyjamas, and the lovely thin white cotton khadi shirts.

Such changes mean gains and losses. The gains are mostly for the middle classes: new Indian-built Japanese cars, a fast new railway down the west coast, American-style banks and investment houses, expensive blocks of flats, high-rise offices above the shanty towns. The losses are of beautiful and characteristic things that used to seem typical – like the heavy teak dugout boats on the Cochim backwaters, now abandoned and rotting because lorries are quicker; or the dilapidated tin-roofed Raj houses in the hill stations, unloved by the people who could afford to look after them, and likely to survive only as curiosities.

Looking at India is an intense experience: there is so much to see that is beautiful, strange and touching. But it is also troubling and even shocking: life there can be puzzling, incomprehensible, dangerous and spectacularly unfair. This is, of course, true of Europe too, but not to the same degree; and here at home, we are used to it and no longer notice it. India is most beautiful where it is still catching up. The prettiest things there are those that remind us of our simpler past; the saddest are those that repeat mistakes that in Europe we have already made.

There are many things I shall miss: scalding railway platform tea poured into throw-away brown earthenware cups; roadside stalls, on the ground or on barrows with four bicycle wheels; milk drunk from a newly cut coconut; the aerial agility of the kites and the lovely effortless gliding of the vultures; the incredible loads of hardware balanced on the backs of bicycles; the groups of yellow autorickshaws waiting for passengers in the shade under the trees; the sight of a bullock cart jammed tight with farm workers, or people equally tightly packed on the roof of a bus; families of four on a scooter; elephants carrying logs or bundles of their own fodder along the road; the snake charmers; cold fresh lime sodas when one is tired and thirsty; the taste of a roadside omelette made with fresh onion; the big spreading trees with their hanging curtains of trailing creepers; the openness and friendliness of young Indians; the unselfconscious attitudes in which people stand or crouch as they wait for a bus; fires by the road at night in the winter, and the blanketed figures gathered around them.

India is not a comfortable place – it is too strange and too many-sided for that. But it is an intriguing and thought-provoking one. Going there entails surprises, delights and shocks – more so than in any other country I've been to. Its natural landscapes are beautiful, its monuments and artistic treasures magnificent, its people fascinating. But there are more and more of them using up even India's vast resources; its once peaceful secular structure is threatened by sectarian struggles and suddenly looks fragile; the middle classes are getting richer, the poor are not. The country is changing itself very fast and not always for the better; anyone who feels tempted to see India should go quickly.

Bundi

Lodi Tombs

Delhi

First impressions are vivid and accurate, and Delhi is where I formed mine: of a fast-growing city with smog and traffic, suburbs and wide leafy dual carriageways, and concrete flyovers with people living under them; of camel carts and autorickshaws and indestructible old Morris Oxfords called Ambassadors; of chirping squirrels, fork-tailed kites and silent vultures; of satellite dishes and Wimpy bars. Delhi is a place where lawnmowers are pulled by teams of bullocks, where new hotels and offices are overlaid on the remains of older regimes – of Lutyens and Baker (see page 33), and the Victorian administrative buildings of the Raj, and of the splendidly domed mosques and tombs of the Mughals.

There are several distinct Delhis, some geographically separated, others simply built on top of earlier ones. Old Delhi or Shahjahanabad is a warren of narrow streets and lanes and bazaars, full of teeming life and bustle and struggle, with its main wide thoroughfare of Chandni Chowk and its two great monuments, the Friday Mosque or Jami Masjid and the Red Fort. To its north is the Ridge and the rather faded area associated with the nineteenth-century Raj, and still full of the bloody and dispiriting relics of the Mutiny. To the south is New Delhi, the diplomatic, administrative and commercial region. This is an area of fast growth, vastly busier and more built-up now than when I was first here in the sixties. Its central features are Connaught Place, the commercial and tourist centre, a once beautiful circle of turf and foliage ringed by elegant colonnaded shops which are now dwarfed by tall and undistinguished office blocks; and, to the south, the grandiose Imperial layout: the President's residence, the Secretariat, the Parliament building, and Rajpath, the monumental avenue that stretches away to Lutyens' great archway, India Gate. Beyond it lie the Diplomatic Enclave, once a sort of open garden city but now much filled in with development; vast areas of burgeoning modern suburbia; and the airport.

While the most lively and irrepressible bits of Delhi are the parts like Janpath, teeming with life and commerce – street traders, money-changers, shoe-shine boys, touts, beggars, other tourists – the places I like best are quieter and older and more remote: either – like the ruins of Tughluqabad – out in open country that Delhi has not yet quite absorbed, or hidden away – like Khirki Masjid and Begampur – amidst obscure suburbs, and little visited. I especially like the gardens and open spaces like the Purana Qila and the Lodi Tombs. These are by no means deserted – one is surrounded by picnics and cricket and soft-drinks sellers and impromptu athletics and decorous flirtations – but they are grassy, relatively peaceful, full of trees and thickets, birds splashing about on the well-watered lawns, and splendid and unfamiliar buildings with vultures perched on their onion-shaped domes. At dusk, the place begins to empty, kites and vultures glide softly in to roost in the branches of the bigger trees, and the few remaining figures begin to look shadowy and mysterious in a fading light.

Khirki Masjid and Tughluqabad

The shabby and unassuming village of Khirki lies to the south of Delhi. Hidden within it, slightly off the road and unknown to taxi drivers, is a remarkable building which looks more like a moated fortress than the mosque that it really is. From outside, the atmosphere is strikingly austere, yet rural, with village children and youths and the soothing sounds of black buffaloes breathing, lowing and farting – a peaceful left-over, like one of those farms that have somehow survived as London has spread outwards, as Delhi too is doing. The square mosque is built in two storeys; there are basement cells within the ground-floor arches; the main mosque, occupying the first-floor level, is reached by the arched bridge over the dry moat. The interior is strange and beautiful, and remarkably well thought out: a pillared courtyard divided and subdivided into many small squares, in part open to the sky but mainly covered with low, flat domes. Many of these are now full of clusters of bats, whose incessant irritable chattering and squabbling fills the air while their black, sour-smelling droppings have formed big dome-shaped heaps on the floor beneath.

No one came into the mosque while I sketched inside, apart from two or three boys in yellow shirts who watched me and asked for cigarettes. The mosque was built in 1380, or about fifty years after the fortress of Tughluqabad: in its curious isolation, it is one of the places I like best in Delhi.

After some days of drawing in Old Delhi, permanently ringed by good-natured but determined onlookers, I was unprepared for the rather sinister early morning solitude of the old fortress of Tughluqabad, beyond the southern outskirts of the city. One enters the rocky site through an arched opening in an immense outer wall, strengthened by bastions, only to be faced by the further bastions of an inner citadel. I made my way up to one of these under the silent and disconcerting gaze of a number of vultures; it was only when I clambered up to the topmost tower of the fortress, slightly higher than the bastion opposite, that the birds glided warily off, only their watchful heads moving a little. There were a few labourers at work on restoring the walls, and carrying sand and mortar in baskets on their heads; half of them were women. Someone was coughing from a shady recess in a stone wall: after a while, the person coughing emerged, wary and dusty and red-bottomed – a monkey. The only other living things were the kites, the hoopoes, and the many green parakeets, in bullet-headed and hurried groups.

Tughluqabad was the third of the seven cities of Delhi, dating from 1321 to 1325; it is still the most remote of them. Even so, from its heights one can see the new city creeping up on it, with its pylons and tall chimneys rising out of the grey heat haze.

Khirki Masjid

Tughluqabad

...e Jami Masjid

The Jami Masjid or Friday Mosque, the largest in India, is Old Delhi's most splendid monument: built by Shah Jahan in 1650–56 on a rocky outcrop, high above the old city and the Red Fort. The main, or eastern, entrance is reached by a long straight road, very smelly in parts, but when you get to the top of the steps the great wooden door is closed: it is for kings only. But there are two other gateways, each at the head of flights of steps, to its 100-metre square courtyard. At eight in the morning there are as yet no European visitors; everyone in sight is local, in character, beautifully and traditionally dressed. The place is being tidied up; carpets are being pushed along on trolleys; a sweeper is at work with a broom which he swings continuously round him on the end of a rope; there is an occasional startling whirring noise as all the myriad pigeons suddenly take flight, to settle on the marble domes. I had earlier climbed up one of the minarets to look down on the huddled city and the Fort. At 12.30 the minor streets that surround the mosque's rocky plinth are full now of pavement car and scooter repair workshops, black and greasy but clearly quick and efficient. Nothing mechanical seems beyond repair here. The kind of energy and ingenuity that around the Pacific basin is directed to manufacture, is in India turned to maintenance. The autorickshaw man who drove me back to Maidens Hotel wore a Muslim cap on his shrewd, skinny and vulture-like head.

Jami Masjid

954

4 0021695

Qudsia Garden

The Qudsia Garden and North Delhi

The fine western gateway to the large
Qudsia Garden in North Delhi is agreeably
run-down – time-worn but not in ruins.
Qudsia Begum was a dancing girl who
became the wife of Muhammad Shah. The
garden she laid out in about 1748 is the
prettiest place in North Delhi, an area
north of the Red Fort and towards the
Ridge, known as the Civil Lines. It is
particularly associated with the early years
of the Raj and, depressingly, with the
Mutiny. The Qudsia Garden has only
peaceable associations, but grimmer relics
of the early Raj and of the Mutiny abound
nearby. Two fine gateways stand out: Delhi
Gate at the southern entrance to
Shahjahanabad or Old Delhi, and Kashmiri
Gate at the northern. This is not far from
a similar fortified building bang in the
middle of the road: the remains of the British
Magazine, blown up in 1857 at the outset
of the Mutiny to keep its contents out of the

mutineers' or freedom fighters' hands. Not
far away is the pretty canary-coloured
St James' Church of 1836 – only twenty-
one years before the Mutiny – built by the
half-Scottish, half-Indian Colonel James
Skinner. He also founded Skinner's Horse
Cavalry whose uniforms were of the same
bright yellow colour.

The Mutiny Memorial or Ajitgarh now
commemorates the fallen on both sides in
that tragic encounter: its surrounding
garden was occupied when I was there by a
party of visitors on a Historic Delhi walk.
Nearby are the remains of the Pir Ghaib
– a dilapidated Mughal building just
clinging on in the shadow of present-day
concrete. The ring road east of the Red
Fort makes its way as best it can under a
variety of perilously low and battered-
looking bridges, between the Fort and a
big power station which gives this part of
Old Delhi a practical but unromantic air.

20

Delhi Gate

St James' Church

The Magazines

Kashmiri Gate

Old Delhi

Mutiny Memorial

Pir Ghaib

Old Delhi

The Red Fort and Begampur

The most arresting sight in Old Delhi is the long and lofty moated wall of red sandstone that surrounds the Red Fort or Lal Qila. The main entrance is the Lahore Gate on the west side. In front of it, and separating it from the bustling street life of Chandni Chowk and the rest of Old Delhi, is a wide expanse of open ground, empty and partly grassy when I first saw it many years ago, but now bare and given over to parking for the coaches, taxis, cars, buggies, autorickshaws and cycle-rickshaws of the visitors to the Fort. This great space is fascinating for the life it contains: drivers and cyclists talking and resting as they wait for a fare, or bargaining, or tipping an autorickshaw over at an angle to repair it as its passengers vanish into the Fort.

The wall and its gate are subtler and more decorative than at first glance, and the gate is indeed very pretty, its bastions delicately arcaded and topped by the pretty serrations of pointed battlements or merlons, and the variously sized chatris or domes along the skyline, shaded by their sloping chajjas.

On the rampart in front of the gate, and striking a different note, is a military saluting base. And once one is inside the Fort and past the vaulted bazaar just within the entrance, the place becomes a curious and uneasy mixture: splendid and historic Mughal buildings side by side with working barracks. The whole was much vandalised by the British at the time of the Mutiny, and enormous Victorian barracks

overshadow the delicate Mughal mosques and audience chambers. They were taken over at Independence and are now maintained by the Indian Army in the unappealing military idiom of whitened paving stones, polished brass and hand-painted signs, just like Tidworth or Aldershot.

Distractions take many forms; even in the outlying village of Begampur to the south of the city, it is not surprising that the almost rural peace is broken by blaring amplified music. Even so, the Begampur Mosque still gives a compelling feeling of an earlier age – its immense square paved and empty but for some children and three or four goats. This drawing was made from the roof of the cloisters, up in an odd world

Begampur Masjid

of domes above the dilapidated chajjas or
sloping eaves, and looking across to the
fine prayer hall. Screaming groups of green
parakeets shot past into the nearby trees;
sparrows too, oddly familiar in these
strange surroundings; small striped
squirrels chattered; the children came and
looked at my drawing. Delhi may be
reaching out and preparing to envelop
Begampur entirely, but this place is still
a magical remnant.

Baksh Bagh, the Red Fort

Humayun's Tomb

Humayun's Tomb is striking both for the perfection of its richly decorated structure and for the formal beauty of the well-ordered garden that surrounds it. The pattern of red sandstone and white marble, the skilful disposition of arches of various sizes, and the grace of the central dome (double-shelled, like St Paul's) make it a splendid and accomplished building – even though, when finished in 1565, it was in a new and unfamiliar style, and thus really the first important Mughal monument.

The big, formally placed trees continue and amplify the carefully ordered disposition of paths and lawns.

The steady flow of visitors adds movement and life, but the groups of gardeners were more interesting: men and women, tending the flowers or taking a midday break with cards and conversation, while the mowing bullocks and water buffaloes were unharnessed for a brief rest. There were many bulbuls and crows and hoopoes, their crests springing up like jack-in-the-boxes when they were surprised or nervous.

Humayun's Tomb lies near the edge of the city and from its terrace one has a sense of the adjacent country. Many of its features – the surrounding plinth or podium, the octagonal tomb symmetrical on all four sides, the fine dome, the restrained decoration, the square formal garden around it, the grand arched gateway – are repeated in the Taj Mahal at Agra, of which it was in important ways the precursor.

Humayun's Tomb

Zinatul Masjid

The Zinatul Masjid and Old Delhi

The Zinatul or Ghata Masjid stands on the city wall at the grubby south-western corner of Old Delhi. It looks like a scaled-down version of the busy Jami Masjid, except that, when I was there one Friday afternoon, there was hardly anyone else to be seen; only a few children, a busload of students, and the good-natured Imam in charge. Shoes may be worn in the foreground but not beyond the line of rubble. The arched prayer hall, here as in most mosques, looks a tempting and restful place, with people enjoying the shade or sleeping on the mats: indeed, the mosque's chief practical appeal seems to be as a decent and restful place to escape from the turbulent activity of the pavements of Old Delhi. Its aesthetic appeal is in its simple but perfect arrangement of arches, minarets and domes, and in its delightful alternation of red sandstone and black and white marble.

Even on a Sunday morning when all the shops are closed and shuttered, there is plenty of activity in Old Delhi's smaller streets and alleys – cows wandering unchecked, dogs sleeping, people visiting or going off by cycle-rickshaw, which is the only quiet and practical way – apart from walking – to get through the narrow passages of the old city. Pigeons and kites perch on the unbelievably tangled electric cables and telephone wires that darken the sky, and one or two monkeys quietly go about their business safely out of harm's way and out of human reach among the bilingual notice-boards and name-plates.

But along Chandni Chowk, the main street of Old Delhi, Sunday seems to impose fewer restrictions on commerce, and one can squat on the ground to be given a shave or get a haircut, or have one's shoes elaborately cleaned – complete with water

sprinkler and specially matched pigments added to the polish – just as on a weekday.

At first glance these small streets look a muddle, narrow and twisting, dark and overhung. But they also seem cool, clean and practical, orderly and safe. I enjoyed drawing there. A couple of young architects told me that this shaded, warren-like existence was the right one for the northern India climate, preferable to le Corbusier's modern concrete at Chandigarh (see page 52) with its extravagant and European spaciousness.

Picking one's way through Old Delhi on a weekday is like wandering through an old-fashioned opera set: archways, balconies, vistas, unexpected changes of direction, pitfalls where the road is up. Merchants spread out silks or potatoes on the ground and sit beside them; rich women come and shop as if at Harrods.

NIPU & KA(PM) ASSOCIATES
CHARTERED ACCOUNTANTS

Old Delhi

The Jantar Mantar and the Purana Qila

The most bizarre structure in New Delhi is the Jantar Mantar: a sophisticated observatory, yet one without any glass or metal, electronics or satellite dishes. Its curious circular, segmental, hollow hemispherical and triangular structures were built in 1724 by Maharaja Jai Singh II in order to read accurately the angles of the sun, moon and stars. In India, astronomy and astrology were closely bound up, and concerned with the precise measurement of what you *could* see, and with the earth's own position. Thus, on the tallest and most striking of these structures, the Samrat Yantra or 'supreme instrument', the angled hypotenuse is parallel to the earth's axis, the quadrants on either side parallel to the plane of the equator. These durable but often restored buildings can be entered, explored, descended into, or climbed up, though one must watch one's step. It is a good place for children to play in, and the pleasant gardens that surround it are a popular place to relax in. These odd structures must until recently have looked lofty and impressive, silhouetted against the Delhi sky. But now, beyond the protecting line of beautiful palm trees, they are encircled and upstaged by the much taller offices, hotels and institutions of the newer Delhi; and inevitably the original isolated majesty of the Jantar Mantar has been reduced and cut down to size.

By contrast the Purana Qila or Old Fort stands prominently on an eminence just to the east of New Delhi. It looks awe-inspiring. One enters it through a massive fortified gateway, but inside, it is a pleasant grassy place to spend an hour or two, well planted with palms and other trees. The Qila-i-Kuhna Masjid or mosque is the most interesting of its buildings. It was built in 1541 by Sher Shah, in marble and sandstone, and in a style which combines both Islamic and Indian elements: in its corner stair turrets are Islamic pointed arches with Hindu brackets under them. The gardens of the Purana Qila attract many people: there is much lying on the grass and gentle hugging, and some energetic jogging.

Safdar Jang's Tomb [overleaf] has much in common with Humayun's; but it was built two centuries later, and is decorative and full of detail and a bit fussy where Humayun's is austere and simple.

Jantar Mantar

Qila-i-Kuhna Masjid

28

Safdar Jang's Tomb

Mughal and Imperial Domes

Delhi's skyline was once made up of graceful Mughal domes and minarets rising from foliage, as London's was of spires above leafy squares and terraces. The domes did not then have to be big or tall to be arresting: the Mausoleum of Isa Khan is low-set, octagonal and elegant.

At present, when big new buildings are mushrooming all over New Delhi, the great Lutyens dome on Viceroy's House or Rashtrapati Bhavan remains the one truly distinctive, unmistakable and unique feature of the city skyline. It is an original and inventive creation, drawing on Indian structures – the stupa-like dome, the sloping chajjas projecting around the drum – yet combining these with European motifs into a memorably individual work.

The Rajpath or King's Way is the wide and splendid ceremonial avenue that runs between India Gate, Lutyens' enormous war memorial arch (now the All India War Memorial) and the vast structures of the two Secretariats flanking the approach to Viceroy's House (Rashtrapati Bhavan). This colossal achievement of imaginative planning represents the core of the Imperial city of New Delhi, first conceived in 1911 when it was announced that Delhi instead of Calcutta would become the new capital of India. It was completed in 1931.

The able team of architects in charge of all this was headed by Edwin Lutyens and Herbert Baker, the latter a fine architect overshadowed by the more unpredictable and adventurous Lutyens. Baker could slip up too: he mishandled the tricky rise in the Rajpath as it approaches Raisina Hill; Lutyens called it 'his Bakerloo'.

I enjoy the long walk along Rajpath, especially the grass and trees and the long ponds or basins at either side of the wide road, mown by bullocks and enjoyed alike by people and wild herons and crows. But on Raisina Hill, hot and exposed, the effect of all the red sandstone magnificence is to reduce everyone to lonely and insect-like insignificance. It looks harsh and inhuman: even totalitarian. The intention was to impose a symbol of Imperial splendour and omnipotence, and Lutyens did this so cleverly that the idea has survived even the Imperial collapse. But to what end? Even when it was being built, there was already something last-minute about it: by the early thirties, the whole Imperial edifice was already tottering. Despite their architectural splendour, it is impossible now to see these buildings except as an extravagant sort of shoring-up exercise – PR for something unsustainable and done for. But the dome is lovely.

Rajpath

Rajpath

Rashtrapati Bhavan

Mausoleum of Isa Khan

The Qutb Minar and Coronation Park

Two tall upright monuments stand outside
Delhi to remind us of past rulers. The Qutb
Minar is to the south, and was built by
Qutb-un-Din Aybak, the first Sultan of
the Slave Dynasty, about 1210; it is taller
than Nelson's column, an extraordinary
survivor and testament to the skills,
imagination and ingenuity of its builders.
It is also very beautiful, in its combination
of bold design and intricate detail. The
pleasant surrounding garden is full of
schoolchildren climbing the low walls or
playing cricket, and grown-ups sitting
under the trees. But one can no longer
climb up inside the Qutb Minar: a group
of people once panicked in the narrow
circular staircase and many of them were
suffocated. This is one of Delhi's greatest
and most visited monuments – every visitor
goes to see it, running the gauntlet of people
selling postcards and guidebooks, peacock-
feather fans and trinkets. Being at the edge
of the countryside, the Qutb Minar feels
timeless and remote, a survivor from a
distant and mysterious world. But the drive
back to Delhi is wholly of the present,
along jam-packed highways, through busy
shopping centres and past big poster
hoardings for newspapers and for
cockroach killers.

Coronation Park is at the opposite side of Old Delhi, far out to the north-east; the past it enshrines is more recent but just as dead. Various statues of British rulers and Edwardian administrators, deposed from their key positions in the centre of Delhi, have been re-erected here in some style, their white marble securely positioned on red sandstone pedestals and arranged in a half-circle round the fine sculpture of George V which once stood on Rajpath near India Gate. The exaggerated majesty of this figure grates a bit now – the image-making is too contrived, too obvious, too overpowering. Yet it is a beautiful and skilful work, the soft material and fur trimmings of the Imperial cloak coaxed in a masterly way out of the hard stone. A patient team of workmen was keeping the place in good trim. I felt rather touched by this correct and magnanimous mark of respect to the old order.

Coronation Park

Qutb Minar

The Lodi Tombs

Seen from the north, the three central monuments of the Lodi Gardens appear connected, unified and majestic. They date from the early part of the reign of Sikander Lodi (1489–1517): the Bara-Gumbad on the left may have been a gateway to the lower central mosque. Though still decorated simply and with restraint by alternating the grey and red stones of the façade, these buildings now look rather plain: splendid in silhouette, but no longer as brilliant as they must originally have seemed. But the dome of the tomb on the right was once covered with blue glazed tiles, earning it the title of Shish Gumbad or Glass Dome.

Lodi Tombs

Connaught Place

Connaught Place is the focal point of New Delhi, its commercial and tourist centre and an important and ambitious exercise in town planning. At its heart is a circular park surrounded by a colonnaded ring of shops, with an outer concentric ring beyond; nine wide roads radiate from it like the spokes of a bullock-cart wheel. It must at its Imperial height have been very beautiful if not very Indian-looking, for it is completely European in architectural idiom: finely plastered arches and columns, grand shops with spacious offices above them, gently curving vistas within its own segments, and long, straight tree-shaded ones along the radial roads.

When I was in Delhi in the sixties it was still, despite its neon ads for Gwalior Suiting and the like, pretty much as it must have originally been in the thirties when it was new: with pavement traders selling beautifully displayed lace, jewellery and fruit in the shade of its colonnaded passages, and with its grassy centre peaceful and intact. It was a lovely place for a newcomer to sit on the grass and take stock, and wonder at the strangeness of the people around. But in the intervening period, Connaught Place has taken some bad knocks. It is still an agreeable small park, where people come to read the paper or play cards or simply lie around. One can buy soft drinks and oranges and bananas from beautifully dressed women, keep at bay the persistent shoeshine boys and the would-be masseurs and ear-cleaners, and watch the crouching sweepers as they tend the grass. But the grass now covers a large underground market, the Palik Bazaar, and an underground car park; and although from time to time one may glimpse a cart pulled by a camel, or a dusty-looking elephant, Connaught Place is noisy and smoggy from a whirl of taxis and autorickshaws.

When one is newly arrived from London, still jet-lagged and disoriented, even a Wimpy bar looks comfortingly familiar and safe – like a McDonalds in Moscow. The arcades outside it are full of money-changers and touts for the various emporia nearby, and acres of parked autorickshaws. For short journeys these three-wheelers are convenient and cheap; exhilarating but alarming, like bumper cars; one feels very vulnerable to the jagged and torn bumpers of buses and lorries as they whisk past. Some autorickshaws are dirty and shabby, others are lovingly polished and dusted at every momentary stop. There is a horn with a rubber bulb to the driver's right and a meter, seldom switched on, at his left; and there is a starter lever on the floor, which needs a vigorous yank. This lever is in frequent use, as the engine often stops at lights – perhaps on purpose, for economy. At night,

Connaught Place

Janpath at Connaught Place

for the same reason, autorickshaws are often driven without lights. Many have decorous pin-ups pasted inside. The drivers, like Delhi taxi drivers, vary wildly: some are friendly and knowledgeable, with good English and a good understanding of the sights; some are energetic and piratical, like New York cabbies; others speak little English, can't guess where you want to go, and often don't know the way.

One is never alone for long in India; and since people are friendly and curious, an artist is seldom short of distracting and fascinating company. Even if observed silently for a few moments at first while being absorbed, the familiar routine of questioning soon begins: 'What is your name? – from which country? – are you a drawing master?' (never simply an artist,

which appears here to be an unknown occupation). Now and then a small child will watch what one is doing, silently and intently, for perhaps an hour at a stretch. But bigger children and grown-ups crowd round the artist, blotting out the view, with a mixture of friendliness, curiosity, persistence, stubbornness, and if necessary self-righteousness, quite deaf to entreaty: 'Please don't disturb me!' – 'I'm not disturbing you' – 'But you *have* disturbed me – stopped me working!' – 'I have *not* disturbed you – give me one pen, one rupee.' There seems no way of avoiding these exchanges except to sit stony-faced and unheeding, and even this cold, unfriendly response takes some concentration which would be better spent on the task in hand or, abandoning it, in proper conversation.

The North and the Himalayas

In the north the Himalayas provide India with a beautiful boundary: one which it is inconvenient if not impossible to cross. In consequence, the four northern places I have visited – Srinagar in Kashmir, Leh in Ladakh, Shiimla in Himachal Pradesh, and Darjeeling in West Bengal – all have something remote, outpost- and frontier-like about them; and in appearance – faces, manners, clothes – their people seem to belong to central Asia rather than to India. In some ways these places are too frontier-like for comfort – I had been to Kashmir in the sixties but was discouraged from returning there recently, it now being thought too dangerous.

In Leh, the highest of these capitals, where some visitors get altitude sickness, the mountains are on your doorstep. The most characteristic landscapes include a Buddhist monastery or gompa, perched on an outcrop of rock against a backdrop of forbidding but enchanting snowy mountain ranges. The people look very fine – warmly and picturesquely clad in sheepskins and blankets, their faces tanned a deep red; the market women spinning by hand as they wait for customers. There is a pervasive Indian military pressure here – flights by big military jets and heavy gunfire in the valleys – but nothing at all to remind one of the Raj: this is an Indian outpost, not a hill station.

Shiimla was the archetypal hill station and a sort of flagship of the Raj. In Shiimla, though the town is itself hilly and fairly inaccessible, the proper mountains are some distance off – a remote but compelling presence away to the north. Here, despite an energetic and rampaging free-for-all of new building without any apparent checks, architectural echoes of the Raj are still all-pervading – tin-roofed wooden bungalows, the garrison church, the Mall where once Indians were not allowed to set foot, banks and bookshops and the pretty Gaiety Theatre and, of course, the big, corrugated-tin military HQ. Victorian schools and beautifully fretted wooden blocks of flats sit alongside the video shops and the travel agents of the new Shiimla. But many of the pretty old Raj houses are falling to bits, or have burnt down, some accidentally, others (I was told) not. Times here have changed. It is traffic-free at the centre: cars have to be left outside. What threatens the charm of the place now is its evident booming prosperity, in which the spaciousness and bosky openness of the older Shiimla is being filled in with uninspiring and second-rate concrete structures without style or quality. Of course, if one puts this point of view to a local, the reply is 'How very British of you to think so.'

In Darjeeling, the high Himalayas appear or withdraw into the haze tantalisingly and unpredictably. Here, the past has survived more unscathed and more charmingly than in Shiimla. Darjeeling is pretty and fresh and very steep: the characteristic sight is of people staggering uphill under cruel-looking loads of luggage, merchandise, wood, or cans of water, the weight taken by a headband. It has an extremely pretty Victorian hotel, the Windamere [sic], and some famous boarding schools. The airport is three hours' drive away; it is reached by road or by a splendidly engineered narrow-gauge railway.

Hillsides near Shiimla

Phyang Gompa

Leh, Phyang and Sheh

Leh is surrounded by mountains, snow-
covered or with at least a dusting of it; a
little snow was falling on the way to Phyang
monastery some ten miles away. Phyang is
isolated, off the road and surrounded by
bare fields whose stony walls are topped by
prickly bundles of dried thorn to keep
animals off. There were many steps up to
the monastery, a solid and austere-looking
block which contained an open courtyard
surrounded by terraces and balconies, with
doorways out of which peeped boys' faces.
I suppose some of them will become monks
when they grow up. Apart from them there
were only two people in sight, both monks.
One showed me the holy rooms of the
monastery. The other sat outside on the
terrace making little votive figures about
three inches high out of thick barley dough;
later they would be brightly painted. Seeing
that I was interested in this process, he also
made me a mug of cold thin gruel of the
same flour; just fresh water and the barley
from the fields below. It had no special
taste but was as fresh and pure a
nourishment as one could imagine. I drew
both men (see page 47); they seemed to
think it a compliment. Tashi, the guide from

Leh, said that as an artist I had a reason to
stay there longer than most visitors, and
I felt lucky. No other visitors appeared.

South of Leh the landscape widens out
into a plain through which the Indus river
flows; it is flanked by mountains and rocky
crags, one [opposite] topped with
fortifications, others with gompas. Here is
an extraordinary barren expanse of sand,
dotted with innumerable small white stupas
or gortens; not a blade of greenery is to be
seen [see overleaf]. Suddenly a hare races
past, scattering sand and stones: what can
there be for it here in this arid waste? There
are a few donkeys on the road, but little else;
the lines of willows are bare and wintry and
it is hard to imagine this bleak landscape
in summer, with green trees and growing
crops. There are curious square ponds,
separated by stone causeways. Nearby,
there is a vertical rockface by the
roadside: unremarkable until one notices
that it is covered with fine, incised images
of people and animals – a lion, an elephant,
a bird. It is a beautiful and unexpected
element in this rural scene, standing there
by the road like a hoarding for perhaps
thousands of years.

Phyang

Leh

42

mountain near Sheh

Stupas near Sheh

Sheh Gompa

Tikse Gompa and Leh people

The Tikse Gompa or monastery stands
in the bleak Indus valley, surrounded by
snowy mountains, a few miles south of
Leh. This is a cold and lunar landscape.
The small Ladakhi boy [opposite] had been
watching me draw for a while, and also
had a good look at the things in my worn-
out canvas drawing bag: various fountain
and dipping pens, inks, a watercolour box
and a screwtop plastic water pot, a tin box
for brushes, a sponge and some tissues,
some pencils that I hardly ever used, and
a bottle of drinking water. This last was
unnecessary in rural Ladakh, where
nothing is dirty yet and water still comes
straight from the mountain snow. After a
while some other children turned up, and
to distract them I asked the small boy to let
me draw him; he stood very still for about
three quarters of an hour. The people of
Ladakh are most curiously and
picturesquely dressed: big trousers like
Dutchmen, sheepskin jackets, velvet hats
with pointed earflaps whose tips curl up.

Market, Leh

46

Darjeeling

Darjeeling

At the animated centre of Darjeeling is Chowrasta, the Town Square, where four roads meet – the green-shuttered Oxford Bookshop on the left is a handsome Raj relic. There are many Tibetan refugees among the Sunday crowds. In early April the temperature is that of a warm spring day in England, a nostalgic impression intensified by the sound of bells from the nearby yellow-painted St Andrew's Church.

Darjeeling is very steep, and few of its streets and pathways are level. The prevalent building style is the old tin-roofed, multi-gabled wood and fretwork idiom of all the Raj hill stations – durable, picturesque and splendid where, as at St Joseph's College, it can be well maintained, but elsewhere often looking sadly near the end of its days.

Until 1881, when the miniature railway was opened, anything that came in or out of Darjeeling had to go by bullock cart. The railway has now itself become a picturesque relic, kept going largely for the tourists, its track used between trains by the local people for trundling their own gear about on small hand-trucks. Its highest point, and the world's second-highest station, is at Ghoom, a few kilometres from Darjeeling; not far away is Ghoom

Monastery: the friendly monks there will read (with, it seems, a certain difficulty) from one of the scrolls stacked in pigeon-hole racks round its walls, and they will also blow the long bugles or horns in front of the building: as they do so, pained farting sounds emerge from the instrument.

The most prevalent job in Darjeeling is carrying heavy loads around on your back. Most of it simply water: I was told that the hotels use up virtually all of the town's piped water supply. My guide said it took him three hours' hard work after his job each night to carry his family's water.

Darjeeling is also a sort of spring board for the Himalayas. Tensing, who with Hillary was the first man to climb Everest, was a local Sherpa who made good: his statue and some of his old climbing gear are preserved here, though there are no traces of Hillary. An old and doddery Himalayan black bear and a Siberian tiger may be seen in the zoo. The hilly slopes around the town are covered with tea gardens; if you get up at 4 a.m. you can go to Tiger Hill to watch (with many other people) the sunrise light up the snows of Kanchenjunga [overleaf], which seems in a certain light to float free, high above the earthly skyline.

overleaf: Kanchenjunga from Tiger Hill

Ghoom

Ghoom

Darjeeling

Darjeeling

St Joseph's College

Ghoom

St Andrew's Church

Chandigarh: Secretariat

High Court

Chandigarh and Shiimla

In 1947, Nehru asked le Corbusier to build a brand new state capital for the Punjab at Chandigarh. Le Corbusier's concrete is vast, monumental and indestructible-looking, yet inventive and personal: every feature of it looks individual and often rather quirky, and thus recognisable as his own personal work. His great administrative blocks – Secretariat, Assembly Chambers, High Court – are set down well apart from each other on an enormous expanse of flat concrete which looks like the tarmac of a wartime aerodrome. This impression is enhanced by the various barbed-wire barriers with clothes drying on them, the wooden military checkpoints, the soldiers cycling about, and the fatigue parties tidying up the playing fields. Such irrepressibly makeshift human details chip away at the cold majesty of le Corbusier's

extremely alien conception; yet they also give it some life and make it look human and Indian, which otherwise it wouldn't. I particularly liked a small, elegant, open building with no apparent function, called the Palace of Shadows. What was it for? My guide said 'Nothing', but that hot and exhausted tourists liked it for its shade.

Up in the hills beyond Chandigarh lies Shiimla, full of old buildings that were once equally alien: wooden, prefabricated, with corrugated roofs to throw off snow and rain. This durable style is common to all the hill stations and looks pretty to British eyes, but it is now ageing and hard to maintain [see central Shiimla, overleaf], and is not yet prized as an antique; any space in these towns is now filling with concrete buildings that look like amateurish Corbusier caricatures.

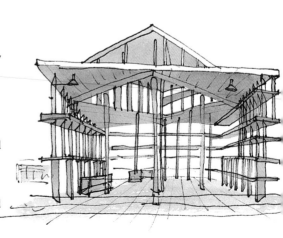

Palace of Shadows

Near Shimla

The Mall, Shimla

Rajasthan

Rajasthan is spectacular, wild and beautiful: a place of extremes. It has savage-looking hill forts and exquisitely painted palaces, pretty lakes and featureless deserts, carefully ordered grid-plan cities like Jaipur and others like Jaisalmer, whose jam-packed streets seem spontaneous and haphazard growths. Rajasthan is distinguished by the beauty of its people and especially by the bright and flowing costumes of the women. There are many local variations of these, which change from city to city: waistcoat-like bodices in Jodhpur, tube-like armbands made of white plastic rings in Jaisalmer. There are glowing and startlingly intense colours everywhere, contrasting with the greys and oatmeal tints of the men's blankets and, here and there, the black gowns of Muslim women.

Rajasthan has many extraordinary palaces: some, like Bundi or Udaipur, are indigenous, ancient, historic and lovely; others, like Bikaner or Jodhpur, have a harder, more academic and more sterile magnificence, betraying a European architect working in an Indo-European style for an unimaginably rich princeling. These princely states exchanged true autonomy for qualified independence effectively under the control of the British, a system which allowed the rulers to become very rich while their subjects remained poor and backward, as in relative terms they still are. The loss of these privileges in the 1970s forced some of the princely rulers to turn their palaces into hotels, often well stocked with funny or touching memorabilia of the old order. Here for a day or two one can enjoy a glimpse of past splendour and its attendant oddities: ballroom floors that can be cranked up to eye level for displays of dancing, fiercely toothed and horned hunting trophies hung on the dining-room walls, a Maharaja's old railway carriage stranded with doors ajar on the lawn outside a fine sandstone portico, old cameras and hi-fi gear, and ugly air-conditioning units projecting from the delicately scalloped sandstone Mughal arches round the windows.

But the buildings I found most interesting to draw were the fine fortresses – Chitor, Jodhpur, Udaipur, and above all Jaisalmer, standing sharply silhouetted above the extraordinary ferment of the old desert town below. Much of Jaisalmer – temples, palaces, fine houses – is contained *within* the fort. Life unrolls here at a more leisurely pace than down in the bazaar; or so at least I thought while drawing the scene opposite, as a whole afternoon seemed to be slipping idly by, unrelished and unimproved by these lazy, low-spirited old men – without even any apparent enjoyment. It was only at the end of the afternoon, when all the others had gone, that the last man told me it had been a 'condolence', a sort of wake; and I felt ashamed of my silly mistake and my insensitivity.

Two experiences remain sharply in my mind. One is the sight of the Pushkar camel fair: the proud and independent people as well as the extraordinary and beautiful animals, odd and individual at close quarters, dignified and graceful at a distance as walking or loping they string across the landscape for fodder, water or exercise. The other thing I will remember is the nobility of an old musician, playing late one evening with four or five others of his musician caste, and then quietly stopping to listen with seriousness and devotion, while the younger men went on playing.

Jaisalmer

Chitorgarh

Padmini's Palace, Chitorgarh

Chitorgarh and Padmini's Palace

From the rather ordinary town of Chitor, with its railway, its underpasses and its wide ancient bridge, the long fortified hilltop of Chitorgarh makes a forbidding and even ominous skyline. The climb up to the hilltop is true to type: steep road, sharp hairpin bends, several fortified gateways. At the top is a long plateau with many temples, two tall towers – the Tower of Victory and the Tower of Fame – and three palaces, including the pretty Padmini's Palace which stands in a tank or small lake towards the southern end of the fortress. The water level was low, exposing the steps beneath the walls at the left. Such geometrically planned steps, offering access to the water at any level and forming complicated repeating patterns of light and shade, are a curious feature of many Indian tanks. During the siege of Chitorgarh in 1303 it was the beautiful and brave Princess Padmini who led the women of the city to their death by self-immolation rather than face capture and dishonour. In all, 50,000 people died.

On the side of the precipice beneath the Samadishvara Temple is another tank, sheltered as it were by a fold in the long curtain wall of fortification surrounding the hilltop, its water deep toned and green and impenetrable. The distant silhouettes of romantically ruined buildings are characteristic of this fierce and warlike region. But its present-day realities are mild and harmless; painted tongas, yellow autorickshaws and ugly Tempos, three-wheelers, crates of Frooti soft drinks and Bisleri soda. There are always some learned guides, intelligent and good-natured Indian visitors (I saw very few Europeans), and the ever-present peasants bearing heavy loads of hay.

Jodhpur

At the edge of the Thar Desert stands
Jodhpur, a big city overshadowed by an
immense lump of rock to which the
Meherangarh Fort clings. A chugging
autorickshaw will take you up as far as its
first gate. Once inside, the road continues
up through six more gateways, at some of
which it doubles back on itself to confuse
and puzzle any intruders. Beautifully
costumed groups of musicians and
dancers await one's arrival at various
strategic points on the way up, wherever one
stops to draw breath and to look down on
the surrounding jumble of cube-like town
houses. Here, as often in Rajasthan, one
is struck by the contrast between the massive
forbidding strength of the fortresses and
the creamy fragile grace of the palaces
they often contain.

This drawing was made in the late
afternoon just inside the first gate, looking
up past the tough inner fortress walls to
the delicately decorated royal apartments.
Vultures wheel serenely in the updraught
above the cliff-like palace walls.

Jodhpur

Bikaner Palace Hotel, Mount Abu

Mount Abu

Mount Abu is Rajasthan's only hill station, set in a landscape of fantastically shaped boulders near a small artificial lake. I stayed in an old and grand hotel, the Bikaner Palace, which was originally the Maharaja of Bikaner's summer home; so spread-out that in my splendid suite the bath took twenty minutes to run hot. The palace was full of triumphant-looking photographs of a previous Maharaja, a fine sportsman, polo-player and pilot. In the palace garden is a small, prettily wooded lake with the painted sign 'Beware of the crocodile'.

Mount Abu is a popular holiday resort. It has the hill station's predictable but rather touching Raj relics – a picturesque cottage-like telegraph office, a tin-roofed church, houses with names like The Glen and Woodland Way, beauty spots called Honeymoon Point and Sunset Point and Toad Rock. But, the place has grown and most of the fantastically shaped crags are now topped by ugly concrete buildings.

Mount Abu: the lake

62

Mount Abu

Udaipur

Udaipur is famous for its splendid Lake Palace Hotel and the enchanting Jag Mandir on Lake Pichola's other main island. But the most interesting place is the dhobi ghat on a narrow arm of the lake, a waterside terrace with steps where people – mainly women and often with their children – do the laundry. They bring heavy loads of washing in baskets on their heads, wash it laboriously and noisily with much heavy slapping which echoes characteristically from the surrounding walls, wring it out and hang it to dry on the iron railings, and finally carry it off again on their heads with majestic, upright grace. This is not only an unvarying and timeless labour but a sociable one as well, with much chatting and slapping and an occasional row. This drawing was made from the opposite bank of the lake; there I found a quiet and inaccessible place by a small temple, where there were only a few children to watch me and, nearby, some priests doing their own washing in the lake. Small fish and plants flourish in its water – indeed, some other parts of the lake look more like cabbage fields. Round the shore are temples, belvederes, some modest Indian hotels and some big shady trees; the water level was high after rain and the place had a romantic Venetian quality. The triple-arched gateway makes a grand theatrical backdrop to the busy and noisy crowds of washerwomen; but if one wants a quieter scene one can wander along the water's edge for some distance, enjoying an almost deserted sequence of small ghats with fine views across to pretty foliage and white buildings, and glimpses of the bigger lake and the backdrop of brown hills that ring the town like the distant landscapes in Umbrian paintings.

Udaipur, Lake Pichola

Jaisalmer

The overnight train from Jodhpur to Jaisalmer leaves about 11 p.m. It travels slowly but steadily; when it gets light next morning the desert landscape is sandy, flat and empty. Jaisalmer is at the end of the line and surrounded by miles and miles of nothing – it feels totally remote. It is a magical and beautiful place, built of honey-coloured stones: a spreading town, densely packed with fine houses, tiny shops and palaces, and entirely dominated by the immense walls and bastions of its great fortress. Its narrow, twisting and mystifying streets are flanked by unbroken rows of shops and small businesses, packed side by side like shoe boxes and not much bigger. The streets are filled with scooters and autorickshaws, hand-carts, cows, goats, cars, and people in beautiful clothes.

The fortress walls look splendid from below, but their structure is better understood if one climbs to the highest rooftop of the palace and looks down on the complex pattern of outer walls and inner bastions, with flat roofs constructed as gun platforms [overleaf]. From up here the town looks like an intricate and formless maze, with the hot, bare desert, stretching far into the hazy distance.

costumes, Jaisalmer

66

Near Jaisalmer

Jaisalmer

Pushkar

Pushkar is built around a small but holy lake: its white buildings, temples and bathing ghats are dismissed by the guidebook as of little interest. But the lakeside scene is fascinating: the steady to and fro of people along the water's edge, the crows and the group of nine waterbirds that patrol the mud as if it were their own private kingdom, the arrival of a string of camels to drink from the holy lake, the lovely play of light on the distant waterside buildings. I arrived in the town as people and animals were assembling for Pushkar's famous camel fair, held on the outskirts of the town at the edge of the desert [overleaf]. This was a good time to see it, as most of the animals had already arrived but the great crowds of visitors were still to come. The fair is a remarkable spectacle – a vast landscape of camels extending as far as one can see. Its nearby slopes are thick with animals, young and old, mostly hobbled with rope; many are prettily decorated with coloured ribbons and favours. With them are their drivers and their families, camel and horse dealers and various suppliers – of green fodder for the animals, of soft drinks and water, snacks and delicacies, music and dancing for the people. The distant landscape is criss-crossed with strings of camels walking or trotting off in search of food or water, or being exercised. The Rajasthani people, here as elsewhere, look very fine: spare, patient, tough, resourceful, intelligent and independent; the clothes of men and women alike are beautiful and striking. The whole scene is a spectacular and almost unbelievable survival from an unfamiliar and romantic past.

Pushkar Lake

Pushkar Fair

Camel fair, Pushkar

Bikaner Fort

Bikaner and Bundi

Bikaner Fort too looks like a magnificent survival, square and impregnable; but outside its great doorway a grand marble statue of a previous Maharajah overlooks a quite extraordinarily scummy and smelly tank. In the Lalgarh Palace Hotel, once the splendid home of the same Maharajah, old oil paintings show this tank as a pretty blue lake, clear and inviting.

The fort of Bundi clings halfway up a mountain. Inside it are beautiful murals, including one whose subject is the same formal garden that one can just see out of the window. This more modest place has *really* survived intact in spirit.

Lalgarh Palace, Bikaner

The Pink City, Jaipur

Central India

Between Rajasthan, Maharashtra, Orissa, Bikar and Nepal, neither northern or southern, eastern or western, are the two big central states of Uttar Pradesh and Madhya Pradesh. These are harder to pin down or characterise than their neighbours, for they have certain things in common with them; yet in them I came across not only many extraordinary scenes and vivid experiences but two of the places in India that I would most like to return to.

The oddest spectacle is the holy waterside city of Varanasi, the old Benares, and of the strange, almost incomprehensible existence, embracing life and death, along its ghats. Here India seems at its furthest remove from Europe: it takes more than an effort of will to fathom what it's about, and to reconcile the mystical preoccupations of the people bathing in the purifying River Ganga, or Ganges, with the ordinary and mundane daily life that surrounds them in the city streets.

At Khajuraho are the famous groups of beautiful and amazingly decorated temples: subtle and complex structures covered with erotic sculptures, works which combine startling subject matter with sensuous observation and assured technique. Khajuraho is also a lovely place in itself: a sort of open-air museum at the edge of a village where the landscape, the heat and one's fellow visitors intensify the interest of the architecture and the sculpture.

Agra is India's Mecca. Agra's Taj Mahal is at least a strong contender for the distinction of the world's most beautiful building; I felt no sense of anticlimax here. And in the nearby deserted city of Fatehpur Sikri one finds ancient monuments of great interest and perfection preserved almost intact – still isolated, and unharmed by later additions.

The city of Gwalior lies in the shadow of its own great hill fort, high up on top of a long and dominating rocky outcrop which recalls the hill forts of Rajasthan, with fortifications and gates, palaces, colossal Jain figures carved in the cliffs, many fine temples, a radio mast and a smart boys' school.

But it is two other ancient capitals – another hill fort and a village palace – that I would most like to see again. Mandu is now barely more than a village on an isolated rocky outcrop, overlooking a wide plain. Away from the village centre it seems rural and even backward, but among its tanks and lakes are a number of fine buildings of great interest and beauty: among them a remarkable mosque adjoining a fine marble tomb; a curious palace with inwardly sloping walls which are supposed to give the beholder a swaying sensation; a romantic and deserted range of ruins along the edge of a quiet tank; and the clifftop pavilion of Rupamati, the beautiful mistress of a sixteenth-century ruler of Mandu. This fairly remote place has not been spoilt or vulgarised in any way.

Orchha is not a fortress but a quite riverside village which, like Mandu, has several fine palaces. The most splendid is the Jahangir Mandir, an amazingly complex square block, symmetrical on two axes; tough, logical and strong in design, yet so gracefully and delicately detailed that one is struck as much by its lightness and its fragile skyline as by its impregnable solidity.

These last two places are far from unknown but they are slightly off the beaten track and in each of them one can see the traces of their past splendour without being distracted by the realities of the present.

Taj Mahal, Agra

Taj Mahal

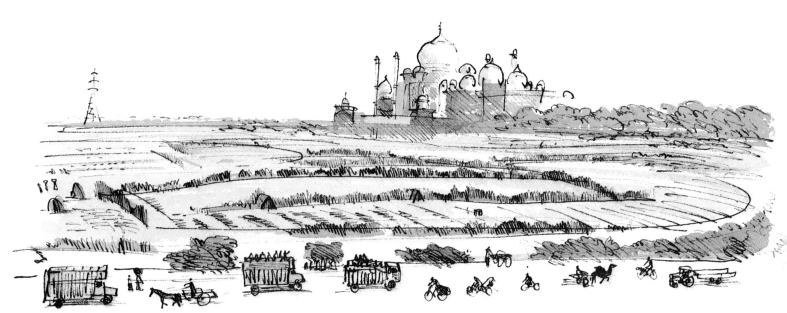

Taj Mahal from Agra Fort

The Taj Mahal

The Taj Mahal is remarkable at any time of day and in any light: gradually taking shape through an early morning mist, blazingly white and incandescent against a blue midday sky, or palely silhouetted in the evening as the light begins to go. Its setting enhances it: the formality of the garden, the long, rectangular pond in which the marble dome is reflected, the lawns mowed by fine oxen, the occasional dark accents of shrubs and trees, and above all the sense of seclusion and peace. This last is unaffected by the stream of visitors whose mood is generally expectant, respectful, and even reverential. Despite the obvious risk of anticlimax, the Taj seems to disappoint no one, and to impress anyone who sees it as a masterpiece. As Edward Lear said: 'Henceforth, let the inhabitants of the world be divided into two classes – them as has seen the Taj Mahal; and them as hasn't.'

The Emperor Shah Jahan (Ruler of the World) built the Taj between 1631 and 1652 as a mausoleum to his much-loved second wife Mumtaz Mahal, who had borne him fourteen children. Shah Jahan had also built much of Agra Fort, a mile away up the river and itself a remarkable assemblage of great Mughal buildings; it had been begun by his grandfather Akbar. Seen from the Agra Fort across the fertile mud flats of the Jumna river, the Taj looks pretty and fragile, its domes translucent and bubble-like. This is the poignant distant view that its builder Shah Jahan had to be content with during his last seven years, when he was imprisoned in the Fort by his son Aurangzeb.

Much of the interest of being in India, even at a place like the Taj Mahal, comes from the faces of the people there. These are given extra fascination by the turbans and beards, which seem to a hatless European as curious as fancy dress or pageant gear. The Jain priest considerately wears a mask to avoid inhaling insects, as much respected as all other fellow-creatures.

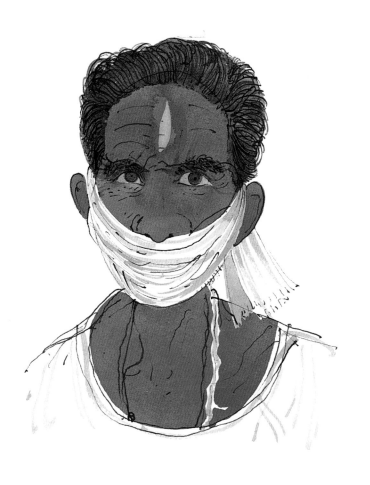

Faces, Uttar Pradesh

Sarnath and Varanasi

Sarnath

The Dhamekh Stupa at Sarnath is the main feature of this pleasant, grassy and wooded place. The Stupa, from the fifth and sixth century AD, is faced with stone below and brick above; its silhouette is recognisable and distinctive. It is important historically because it was here that in the fifth century BC Buddha preached his first sermon. It is now a place of pilgrimage for Buddhists: there are many red- and saffron-robed pilgrims among the monuments, and I made this drawing to the steady sound of half-soothing, half-irritating chanting from a Tibetan monk seated motionless beneath the tree, his shaven head just visible above the low wall. As I drew, a young Buddhist nun from Kerala, in a saffron habit, came to talk to me, with the pleasantly open and confident friendliness characteristic also of Christian nuns in India – as if their habit gave them an assured status and the confidence that their friendliness and openness would not be abused.

The tree, and the creeper which is taking it over, was beautiful on this warm, quiet morning. But Sarnath is only six miles from Varanasi, the old Benares, where peace and tranquillity are inconceivable.

The burning ghat at Varanasi is vivid and unforgettable indeed. The scene seemed to me at first curious and macabre, then interesting and surprisingly businesslike, and in the end touching and moving. In essence it is simple enough. The dead person's body, entirely wrapped in coloured materials and garlanded but still revealing its frail human shape, is brought by the mourning family to the steps leading down to the holy Ganges. Sometimes a drummer or a band comes with them. The body is left at an angle on the sloping steps to wait its turn to be briefly immersed for purification; it is then taken to a funeral pyre of wood on which it is burned for several hours until it is completely consumed. The firewood comes by boat and is unloaded and stacked in neat

82

Stupa, Sarnath

manikarnika Ghat , Varanasi

piles on the bank until needed; this task, and those of laying, lighting, stoking and tending the pyres with long pokers are carried out by professionals, members of the appropriate castes. Other people casually or curiously watch what is going on from upper terraces or from boats on the river; photography is not allowed. Several pyres are alight at once, catching alight or blazing or smouldering. It all seems oddly informal; people and animals wander about, buffaloes and goats nose at the floating marigold garlands, dogs sniff at the ashes, and all is set against a backdrop of temples and houses rising up the steep banks.

Of course one can take, or perhaps try to suppress, a ghoulish interest in a process so unvarnished and so inconceivable in, say, Britain. What is strangest about it here in Varanasi is the mixture of practicality and sheer hard work with the seriousness and emotion in the presence of death – things we keep separate. The practicality is clear enough in the disciplined and economical movements and the detachment of the woodmen with their long poles. The emotion is in one's own mind or glimpsed here and there in the tired, dejected attitudes of the relatives sitting by the steps.

The Daśhashvamedha Ghat [overleaf] is the centre of Varanasi's river-front activity, several hundred metres from the burning ghat. It is at its busiest early in the morning as bathers face the rising sun across the River Ganges, in an apparent combination of devotional ritual, or puja, and the simple celebration of being alive. The long lines of steps are interrupted here and there by small stone platforms, each shaded by a bamboo umbrella, where priests sit to address groups of followers. The priests must vary in popularity or interest, for some of these groups are tiny, while others are too big for the little platforms and overflow onto the surrounding steps. Traders, hawkers, musicians, boatmen, beggars and holy men or saddhus line the steps leading up to the town streets; people look down from the temple terraces. The bigger, shuttered boats are used as houseboats or (I was told) for smoking cannabis; the smaller ones ferry people across the wide river or up and down the several miles of ghats. Mine served me as a peaceful studio, free of interruptions and held steady in the slowly moving stream by an impassive old boatman and a young boy who was doing all the real work.

Deshashvamedha Ghat, Varanasi

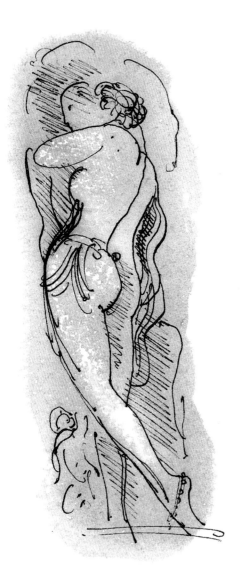

Khajuraho

Khajuraho

Visiting Khajuraho is exhilarating and surprising. Several groups of monuments are covered with detailed carvings of immense vitality, of humans and imaginary creatures. At the mention of Khajuraho, it is the vibrant sexual content that first comes to mind and many of the carved figures are indeed engaged in many varieties of erotic activity, minutely observed – or perhaps imagined – by their eleventh-century sculptors.

But what strikes one equally forcefully is the grace, affection and beauty of these figures – the subtlety and warmth with which their languorous, supple or active gestures have been portrayed, and the skilful delicacy of such things as their garments, their faces, their hair. Grotesque as some of the Khajuraho groups may be, and repetitive as many of their activities certainly are, the dominant impression is one of grace, affection, well-being and high spirits. Many of the finest carvings are to be found round the magnificent tower of

the Kandariya Mahadeva temple [opposite], which is the biggest and most striking of the western group of temples: as mystifying and hard to analyse structurally as it is fascinating in detail.

Khajuraho is pleasantly rural: there are pretty tanks, a village, fertile countryside. The western temples in particular are situated in a pleasant garden amid trees filled with monkeys, with coloured birds and flowers, and enlivened by intelligent and inquisitive groups of visitors. The eastern group temples are interesting for their fine carvings but their setting is not so attractive. The sandy road between the two groups skirts the old village; a newer one, clustering near the western temples, is filled with small hotels and postcard shops and stalls selling the cold mango juice straw drinks which kept me going in the fierce morning sun. Opposite the entrance to the temples, in the shade of a tree, is a pleasant small cafe, the Raja, with a well stocked bookshop next door.

Jahangir Mandir, Orchha

Orchha

Orchha and Fatehpur Sikri

Orchha is a town whose present modest scale – it is hardly more now than a village – is oddly out of kilter with the splendour of its great palaces. The drawing above was made in the small bazaar at the crossroads by Orchha's main gate, sitting on the bench of a tea stall surrounded by good-natured people, with only an occasional passing elephant to lift the scene above pleasantly humdrum village level. But five minutes' walk away, across a fine stone bridge and through a gateway studded with spikes to deter attack by elephants, is an extraordinary building. The fine Jahangir Mandir [pages 88–9] is an early seventeenth-century palace of unusual complexity and beauty. It stands high on a crag overlooking a bend in the Betwa river; its inner courtyard is symmetrical round all its four sides, so that wherever you stand the view looks the same. Its romantic skyline of domes and cupolas is enlivened by the vultures which

glide in to perch on its ribbed domes. Through the delicate pierced stone screens or jalis which surround its upper terrace one can see the lovely twisting river, the tombs beside it, the village and its temples and beyond them all a beautiful and well-wooded countryside. One can stay here in memorable if unpredictable style in a beautiful annexe of the palace; a few yards away is a second palace with many fine wall paintings. The whole experience is delightful and magical.

Fatehpur Sikri, too, is a place whose historical importance far outweighs its present insignificance. The most spectacular single building at Fatehpur Sikri is the Buland Darwaza, the great Gate of Victory through which one enters the mosque. From the bottom of the great flight of steps below it, the gate is awesome in scale. From the terrace at the top of the steps, if one stands back a few feet from the edge and turns round, one no longer sees

the steps, only the platform. One thus experiences the uncanny and vertiginous sensation of being suspended in space. High under the big central arch, as often in such spaces, and in defiance of various attempts to dislodge them, hang glistening black curtains: great swarms of bees. Through the arch, the square courtyard of the Jami Masjid or mosque opens wide and expansive with, at its far side, a most beautiful marble monument. This is the Tomb of Shaikh Salim Chisti, the Sufi saint who had prophesied the birth of Akbar's son, in gratitude for which the city was built. One has to discard one's shoes in the mosque – even uniformed and armed soldiers clump about sheepishly in awkward-looking slippers – and it doesn't feel especially sacred, with its bazaar stalls and fruit sellers and hawkers. But this eager commercial life is vital and picturesque and helps to make this a beautiful and lively place rather than a cold relic.

Buland Darwaza, Fatehpur Sikri

The Tower of the Winds

The road from Agra to Fatehpur Sikri is busy with buses and bullock carts, tongas and taxis, and runs through flat farmland dotted with tall-chimneyed brickworks and carefully domed heaps of dried cow dung. As you approach the deserted city, several groups of dancing bears are cruelly made to caper and cavort over the road in the path of the traffic; two or three vultures perch on the low wall by the city gates.

Fatehpur Sikri was built by Akbar between 1571 and 1585, but abandoned by the end of the century, probably through lack of water – it is well preserved, still isolated, and untouched by later development. Its plan was conceived along Persian lines but the buildings, often original in form and intricately decorated, are in every way Indian.

Some of its most remarkable structures surround the Pachisi court, with its beautifully decorated small square tank. The square building with four cupolas is the Ankh Michauli or treasury. On the squared-out courtyard in front of it the emperor played pachisi, a sort of chess, using his courtesans as the pieces. Today's chess pieces wear bright sarees or cotton dhotis, or the international uniform of blue jeans and back-packs. The tall, open building on the left, topped by a single cupola, is the Panch Mahal or Tower of the Winds, an airy and cool retreat for the women of the court.

Fatehpur Sikri

Mandu

Mandu

Like Orchha, Mandu at first seems small and insignificant. Village-like and well off the beaten track, it is concealed in a remote hilly fastness: from its present-day village street, however picturesque, no one would think it could ever have been the capital of a significant and ancient kingdom. But it was; and, to prove it, Mandu has many fine buildings – some in ruins, some, like the Tomb of Hoshang Shah, in excellent preservation. Hoshang Shah moved the Malwa capital to Mandu on his accession in 1405, when it began 150 years of prosperous independence. His marble tomb is beautiful, in the way the Taj is: simple and logical in conception, its decoration skilful but subordinate to the whole. It stands four-square and solidly based on a low plinth, a perfect building.

The converging side walls of the Hindola Mahal of 1425 are supposed to give the building or the observer a sense of instability, hence its nickname of 'swinging palace'. It too is elegant and accomplished. It is puzzling how the architectural individuality and technical grasp embodied in these two remarkable monuments could have developed and been sustained in this provincial environment. Provincial Mandu certainly remains, despite its beady-eyed foreign visitors. When I went there in mid-April it was already filled with country people who had come for a festival – the women beautiful in brilliant sarees, the men high-spirited in bright new turbans; men and women alike looking like splendid peacocks. A blind drummer was prancing frenziedly at the head of a temple procession, steadied by his more serene companion in a blue and red saree. This was a true country celebration: wherever one looked in the countryside, for miles around, one could see people in ones and twos making their way across the fields to join in the fun, bright notes of red, orange and yellow in the landscape.

Tomb of Hoshang Shah, Mandu

Hindola Mahal, Mandu

The Jahaz Mahal

Jahaz Mahal means Ship's Palace. This long narrow building is situated between two lakes or tanks, which were half-dry when I was there; it must owe its name to its position rather than to its appearance. This drawing is of the main terrace or deck; the smaller pavilions or deck houses were once occupied by the ladies of the harem (indeed, the whole crew of the Jahaz Mahal were women); the arched openings would then have been curtained. This is a cheerful and not-too-serious building, built about half a century later than Hoshang's Tomb and the Hindola Mahal. The ruins further away to the left are all that now remains of the Malwa Sultans' comfortable waterside retreats; these still contain a ruined well, the Champa Baoli, and would have been relatively cool and well ventilated even in the summer heat. Cattle and goats now get what little they can from the dry banks; the two boys fishing seemed to be doing no better. Here, as always in India, much of the interest of the scene comes from the people in it: working or just being there. In England the fields are now deserted.

Jahaz Mahal, Mandu

Rupamati's Pavilion

Rupamati was the beloved mistress of Baz Bahadur, Mandu's ruler from 1526 to 1561. According to legend, Rupamati's end was tragic: she poisoned herself when Baz Bahadur fled from battle with Akbar. This stone pavilion is one of two which adorn the building which bears her name, at the edge of a high ridge overlooking a vast and magnificent landscape, wide spreading and tawny, and watered by the gleaming River Narmada. This is one of the most magical views I came across in India. While I was there the terrace was thronged by country people who had come to the festival in Mandu, and were marvelling at the pavilion's extraordinary situation.

In the village street were parked some Tempos (ungainly and villainous-looking three-wheelers), one or two taxis, and some bullock carts. The bullock cart is still the most vivid and familiar symbol of rural India. Though they are all pulled by the same two animals, they are surprisingly different in wheel diameter and general conformation. Not all these carts are from central India: the ice cart was from Bombay, the lighter covered wagon from Tiruchirappalli in the south; the rubber-tyred version is slowly becoming general. Bullocks' horns are often brilliantly painted. Sometimes their flanks are decorated with stencilled patterns, but they are never painstakingly and individually painted, as elephants often are. However pretty, as works of art, bullocks are mere multiples.

Rupamati's Pavilion, Mandu

Khajuraho

Mandu

Ajanta

Mandu

Ellora

Bombay

Tiruchirappalli

Agra

99

Gwalior: the Man Mandir Palace

Long before one gets to Gwalior one can see the basalt rock of its great fortress rising above the plain. The Man Mandir is the most remarkable of the several palaces within the fortress. It is built at the edge of a precipitous rock, its bastions commanding the town and the plain. From outside and below, its eastern façade looks fierce and forbidding. But its southern façade, shown here, is softer and prettier, decorated with mosaics and brilliant enamelled tiles. Its interior is beautiful but macabre – there are cruel torture chambers as well as beautiful and intricately decorated rooms. The other palaces are partly ruined; with deep stone tanks or step-wells, long perspectives through aligned series of doorways, and hidden passages: they look out over the white walls and dark trees of the city of Gwalior, far below. I went into one small silent chamber which suddenly filled with the chattering and squeaking of innumerable bats, fluttering like moths round my head.

Gwalior

Golconda Fort

Golconda and Hyderabad

Golconda Fort is built on one of those dramatic Indian crags where one can't tell what is cliff and what is wall. As it is also hard to guess how big the rock is, the schoolchildren and the brightly dressed groups of visitors wandering around it and disappearing into its caves and tunnels look like ants. The fine jagged skyline is topped by the citadel and the remains of the royal apartments. It is very dry, and was the most pitilessly hot of the places I visited.

Golconda is five miles from Hyderabad, India's fifth city at whose centre stands the Char Minar or Four Towers, India's second most recognisable building – it appears on a well-known cigarette packet. Through it can be seen the Fruit Vendors' Arch and part of the Jami Masjid. At its base is a splendid fruit and vegetable market, serving people from the Muslim community which in British times ruled a mainly Hindu city. The beautiful black jellabas or yashmaks of the women, whose faces can be completely covered by lowering a small veil like a flap, look like the surgical gowns and masks in an operating theatre.

Hyderabad used to be ruled by the extremely wealthy Nizams, and many spectacular domed monuments to their splendour remain: palaces, the High Court, an enormous hospital, the state legislature, a fine museum. A colossal Buddha is being erected on an island in a lake. It also has a pretty old hotel whose intricate Gothic windows, more appropriate to a Victorian vicarage, sit oddly beneath the palm trees and the neon RITZ sign; and there is a curate's egg of a museum, with beautiful Indian miniatures and poor European sculpture which only looks good when surrounded by enthralled Indians. There are many new blocks of flats: one with a hoarding which reads 'Gardenia Residence: a magnificent abode for the choosy'. It doesn't feel like India's fifth city.

Hyderabad

Char Minar

Cave 19, Ajanta

Ellora and Ajanta

The rock-cut cave temples of Ellora and Ajanta which began as Buddhist and Jain shrines and monasteries have become shrines of tourism. They are revered for their structural ingenuity and artistic imagination, visited and experienced for very different reasons from those that originally brought them into being. They are fascinating and exhilarating places in their own right, but also because of the energy and adventurousness of the people, many of them young, who now throng them.

The caves at Ajanta are cut high up into the cliff-like side of a horseshoe-shaped gorge, with a sparsely covered hillside above them and thick woodland below, reaching down to the boulders and pools of a river; on its far side a similar steep rocky cliff faces them. The surrounding scenery is of great natural beauty, though the access path that serves the caves now is a clumsy concrete affair. One can reach Ajanta by bus or on foot from the nearby village of Fardapur, itself a pleasant base for a day or two's visit.

The astonishing thing about the wall paintings in the Ajanta caves is not just their skill and complexity as compositions but their subtlety and expressiveness – for example, the clarity and assurance with which a sideways glance suggests an emotion or a personality. And this in the fifth century: it upsets the vague artistic timetable that most Europeans take for granted, in which the fifth century is merely part of a long fallow period.

The landscape in which the Ellora caves are set is quite different. They are cut in a long straight hillside, facing west and overlooking a wide plain. Some are simple cells, some are confusing warrens on several levels, interlinked by stairs and passageways cut in the basalt. As at Ajanta, they are remarkable for the complete integration of the structure with the sculpture, which is not a merely decorative addition but is an essential part of the whole. Carved figures graded into different sizes according to their importance are skilfully incorporated into friezes or into groups within the architectural structure; surfaces are intricately decorated, yet with skill and restraint.

The most unforgettable sight at Ellora is the Kailasa cave, a complicated architectural sculpture in itself; for although it initially appears to have been built up within a sort of open quarry in the sloping rock face, the space around it has really had to be cut away block by block, chip by chip, and the whole temple created by removal, not addition. One may wonder, as at the pyramids, if this was a *sensible* project to embark on; the achievement was certainly an astonishing effort of will and of organisation.

The experience of visiting these caves is one of calm and serenity. But when I was there, India was neither peaceful nor serene. I came back from Ajanta to the pleasant small rest-house in the village of Fardapur to see inter-communal rioting and bloodshed at the Ayodhya mosque on television; the buses that came into the village had their windows smashed; for a day or two it wasn't safe to leave Fardapur and go back to the nearest city, Aurangabad, where many people had been killed.

Daulatabad

Ellora is an hour's drive from the city of Aurangabad. Halfway there one passes what must be India's most remarkable hill fort, crowning an immense pyramidal outcrop of granite. The citadel of Daulatabad is surrounded by three concentric walls of fortification, their blackened stones and broken-down bastions stretching far into the thin dry scrub of the countryside. The tall pink minaret on the left is the pillar of victory or Chand Minar, built by Ala-ud-Din when he conquered the fortress in 1296. In the fourteenth century the Sultan of Delhi, Mohammed Tughluq, cruelly – and almost unbelievably – forced the entire population of Delhi to march the 700 miles south to Daulatabad to found a new capital. Many perished en route; the plan failed; and after seventeen years the rest were all marched back.

Sometimes in the Indian landscape it can be hard to tell the difference between human shelters and stacks of crops. The tepee-like tents below belong to an itinerant body of cane cutters, who pitch camp for ten days or so and cut all the sugarcane within reach before moving on. Only one or two women and children, a dog and a buffalo were at home; everyone else was away working.

Cane cutters' tents, Ajanta

The Kailasa Temple, Ellora

At Ellora, a long rocky escarpment overlooks a wide plain, hazy and yellow with the April heat. Many caves have been cut into this rock, pillared and often intricate in structure, some with inner chambers and shrines, others with upper storeys reached by dark stairways or through twisting passageways in the solid rock. The pillars and walls are carved with figures of gods and mortals, animals and imaginary creatures, and are alive with remarkable decoration. In all but one of these caves one has the certainty of being *inside* the rock – surrounded by the solid mass of the hillside and entering it through a hole in that rock, as an animal might enter a lair.

But the most extraordinary monument at Ellora is Cave 16, in great Kailasa temple which seems sunk in a sort of quarry. It needs an effort of the imagination to remember that this great structure, built apparently in the open air, is in reality an enormous monolithic sculpture, and that all the warm airy space around it was once solid rock. The central Kailasa temple is flanked by smaller caves and galleries, reached by tunnels or bridges of solid rock, and supported by uprights so slender that one half expects the rock above to crush them and collapse. It is only when one clambers up the steep paths of the surrounding hillside that one can begin to realise the almost incredible task that faced the people who cut into it.

Kailasa Temple, Ellora

Kailasa Temple, Ellora

Kailasa Temple, Ellora

Ajanta

Indian country women wear traditional clothes which are good to look at but hard to understand if you are drawing them; wound around and across the body and, in movement, free to float wispily and translucently behind, very different from the tubular jeans and shirts into which westerners and younger Indians insert themselves. Returning later to Europe I felt that people dressed for a London February looked more like bundles of warm clothing than gracefully clad bodies, whereas Indian clothes can seem both practical *and* beautiful, like petals.

Country people like these Ajanta women are usually burdened by loads – bags or bundles of produce or shopping, fuel or fodder – or they carry heavy water pots stacked one on top of another on their heads; this last makes for a stately and upright carriage. The evening scene as people return from the fields, by foot or on a bullock cart or perched on a tractor, is timeless and lovely. The bright colours of these clothes add touches of clear red or orange, blue or green to a landscape which is usually simply tawny, taking its colour from the brown earth.

In Calcutta one still sees men pulling rickshaws; it looks rather shocking. But it was only at Ajanta that I ever saw the traditional palanquin in use, carrying a delicate-looking woman up the steep paths outside the caves – performing the role of a more versatile wheelchair.

The Ajanta Gorge [opposite] was being tidied up by early morning sweepers, as I drew it from the viewing point on the opposite bank of the gorge. Few people climbed up to this vantage point: only one or two monkeys enlivened the morning's unusual solitude.

Ajanta Gorge.

HI

fardapur

Ajanta

fardapur

Ellora

Fardapur

People in Fardapur village

The drawings opposite were made as
people in Fardapur village near Ajanta
waited for their buses. Their suppleness,
and the ease and relaxed naturalness of
their attitudes and gestures are Indian
characteristics, apparent also in the cave
sculptures and paintings. No one seemed
either to expect or need a bench to sit on.

In this rural and old-fashioned part of
the Deccan, the men's tent-like white
cotton pyjamas and lunghis and Nehru hats
have not yet entirely given way to jeans
and tee-shirts; they look cool and graceful,
as does the inch or two of back visible
above the securely wound and skirt-like
lower swathes of a saree. Turbans never look
cool but they can be eye-catching, rakish
and individual like the fried-egg look-alike
opposite: sparky assertions of personality.

This particular street has kept its village
character, despite the filling station and the
name FARDAPUR proudly painted round the
stone base of a big banyan tree. The bus
stand, with the tea and soft-drinks stalls
and fruit sellers that cluster round it, is
the liveliest place in the village street: a
good place for drawing if one can stick it out
in such an exposed position.

Ajanta

113

Calcutta and the East

Calcutta suffers from a unique and sensational reputation for spectacular overcrowding, squalor and misery, and the visitor therefore approaches it warily. Parts of it indeed are squalid and run-down; one sees misfortune, drug abuse and misery on its pavements, as one does in Bombay or Delhi, or indeed in London. What I was unprepared for was finding the remnants, admittedly in various states of repair, of so much Imperial and commercial splendour, and discovering it to be a place not sunk in despair but teeming with inventive, intelligent and courageous activity.

In the commercial centre of Calcutta around Dalhousie Square (BBD Bagh) are many extraordinarily grand buildings, set round a big square tank in which children fish and bathe. Not far away there are splendid arched entrances to grand palaces like Government House, guarded now by Calcutta's helmeted, tough and wiry-looking policemen in white battledress. But there are other once-grand gateways now so crumbled away and overgrown that it is hard even to imagine their original purpose. There are pretty churches and pathetic monuments to British grandees – bishops, chief justices – who, like so many of their compatriots, lasted only very briefly in the climate. There is the staggeringly self-confident and smug Victoria Memorial, made out of the same Makrana marble from Jodhpur as the Taj itself; it stands in the middle of a hot and dusty Maidan, which *didn't* once make me think of Hyde Park. There is a splendid new Underground, and there is the astonishing Howrah Bridge of 1943, which with its graceless but indestructible practicality seems an appropriate enough legacy from the final days of the Raj, its lower (or road) deck now a solid traffic jam. My most vivid Calcutta impression is of a morning at the bathing ghat almost underneath the bridge [page 118]. Men were washing and bathing and women were doing the laundry while vultures picked clean the cow's carcase which was bobbing gently down the stream in a reddish patch of water, just off the steps. By now nothing in this scene struck me as disturbing or even odd; it just seemed how things are.

South-west of Calcutta on the Bay of Bengal is the state of Orissa. This includes the temple city of Bhubaneshwar, Konarak with its famous Black Temple, and the pleasant seaside town of Puri – part Indian watering place, part fishing village. Bhubaneshwar is worth visiting for its many interesting and beautiful temples, which are mostly set in open and green surroundings. The countryside around is a flat and fertile landscape of shimmering paddyfields, coconut palms and bullock carts. At Pipli the village houses are decorated with intricate fingerprint murals, dabbed white on the brown walls. Konarak's Surya Temple (the Sun or Black Temple) is much bigger than any of the individual temples at Khajuraho, but like them its walls are surrounded by sculpture, much of it erotic. The treatment and the subject matter are somewhat cruder than at Khajuraho, though the impression may be partly due to its sculptors having used stone which has weathered and crumbled more severely. The whole colossal temple is built to look as though it is a chariot mounted on twelve pairs of beautifully and intricately carved stone wheels.

Royal Exchange, Calcutta

Calcutta's spires and arches

St John's Church (1787), based on the model of St Martin-in-the-Fields, stands in a large grassy churchyard, framed by tropical foliage. This church has been much tinkered with, but it still looks very pretty. In the churchyard are several fine monuments: one to the Black Hole of Calcutta, another to Admiral Watson, and the octagonal tomb (c.1695) of Job Charnock, the English merchant who founded the city. Calcutta's past grandeur is proclaimed by its many fine entrances, often taking the form of Palladian arches flanked by columns of stucco. Sometimes these have decayed spectacularly, with the stucco flaking away, trees taking root in the unsteady-looking brickwork, and cinema posters and ads for smart but long vanished shops holding it together. In front of them, the pavement now offers space to tea stalls, trinket-sellers and fortune tellers with their caged parrots; the roadway is busy with buses, rickshaws, and men carrying baskets of fruit on their heads.

But sometimes the old splendour has been maintained, with Imperial lions still standing guard overhead as if nothing had changed. The old Government House, now Raj Bhavan, has two such arches. Some office buildings too use arches in a baroque or theatrical manner, to enhance a façade or the entrance to a cul-de-sac. Such buildings have not so much decayed as adapted to a more rackety commercial climate than they were built for.

Not far from Raj Bhavan is a patch of ground set aside with railings as the exclusive preserve of a respected colony of rats, whose holes are likewise concealed behind earthy arched entrances.

Job Charnock's monument

Admiral Watson's tomb

St. John's Church, Calcutta

Pavement Stall, Calcutta

gateway

Government House

Rats' Garden

Offices

Bathing ghat, Calcutta

The Howrah Bridge and the Victoria Memorial

Howrah and its big railway station are linked to Calcutta by the spectacular Howrah Bridge, the city's most distinctive sight. Beneath the Calcutta end of it is a beautiful vegetable and flower market, in the midst of a bustling but shabby area. The bathing ghat is busy during the morning: almost as crowded as the ghats at Varanasi, but with no apparent religious ritual involved, simply a natural resource being fully used. There is a constant to and fro of river traffic – passenger boats and cargo craft, sailing and powered. The bridge itself is always laden with traffic. It was built in 1943, remains useful and sturdy, and has the curious unselfconscious beauty of structures that were never meant to be beautiful at all.

The Victoria Memorial certainly was meant to be both beautiful and impressive, and so it is – in the manner of the Parisian monuments whose purpose is to overwhelm. It stands in magnificent isolation on the long Maidan; other aspects show it reflected in long basins of water, framed by arches, or half-masked by big trees. It was built in 1921 by Sir William Emerson, with great skill and accomplishment, and it looks what it is: a good building of its period, but without Lutyens' power to surprise and amaze. Between them the bridge and the memorial represent the two polar extremes of what Britain left behind in India: the one a useful artefact, the other a marble statement of faith in the dream of Empire.

Calcutta has less uplifting memorials to its vanished colonial past. Many once elegant courtyards are now in an advanced state of picturesque decay, their balconies broken down, their plasterwork crumbling, their large arched doorways opening onto squalid squats; yet still possessing an echo of grandeur and spaciousness. These deserted squares are tucked away off the streets, which are packed with traffic and energy.

White-backed vulture

Victoria Memorial

Courtyard

Calcutta thoroughfare

BBD Bagh and GPO, Calcutta

High art and popular craft

The splendidly domed General Post Office (1864–8) stands on the west side of Dalhousie Square, now BBD Bagh, on the site of the original Fort William and the Black Hole of Calcutta. It is a handsome monument to public enterprise, something still respected in India; the square in front of it, surrounded now by busy traffic and tramways, is still a pleasant place where people can fish or sit in peace under the trees at the water's edge. Nearby is the enormous Writers' (clerical workers') Building, once the headquarters of the East India Company and thus the early hub of British commercial administration. To my right as I drew was St Andrew's Kirk of 1818, again skilfully and elegantly based on St Martin-in-the-Fields, with a handwritten 'God Loves You' above the door and monster posters for Amul Butter 'Top of its class . . . full marks in every examination', and the Indian Banks Association 'Dedicated to Customer Satisfaction' in its forecourt. At my back was the scene on page 114.

The handsome courtyard is that of the family home of the Bengali poet Rabindranath Tagore: as a boy he acted in his own plays under the arches on the left. The place is now an art school, and well preserved; but I saw the remains of other fine houses which had fallen on worse times. Some of these were painfully, even comically, evocative of a vanished past.

One of Calcutta's surprises is the vigour of its traditions of craftsmanship and popular art. There are for example many studios, open to the street, where one can follow the development of street sculptures of familiar Hindu subjects. The works begin as men (or gods) of straw, boldly and expertly modelled and bound with twine, to which a clay finish is later added; finally this is brightly painted. The completed piece is set up in the open air and left to take its chance until time and weather reduce it again to its original clay and straw. There are two remarkable aspects of this strange process: the gestures and graceful movement so skilfully suggested by the men working with straw, which looks an intractable material; and the interest taken in them by people who come to watch them being first unveiled in the studio.

Tagore's house, Calcutta

Starting the figure

Completed straw figures

Adding the clay surface

Completed group

Bhubaneshwar

There are several groups of temples at Bhubaneshwar, some with delicate and exquisite carvings, others of more interest for their setting, amid trees or beside a tank where the priests bathe and wash their bicycles. The great Lingaraja Temples are reserved for Hindus; other people may only climb to a platform and gaze at them over the surrounding wall. This gives them an added allure. Orissan temples are generally made up of two distinct elements, one short and squat, one taller. The squat one, entered first, is the squarish *mandapa* or outer columned hall, covered by a pyramid roof. The second, the inner chamber or sanctuary, is covered by a tall curvilinear tower, the *rekha deul*, and capped by an *amalaka*, a circular and ribbed gourd-shaped feature, supported here by crouching lions. On top of this is a small pot-shaped finial. Although guides must have told me the names of these various components at the time, I immediately forgot them and have had to look them up since. Knowing the names, and what goes on inside, makes it easier to understand these unfamiliar structures.

The figures carved on the smaller temples are of unusual charm: without the erotic intensity and curiosity of Khajuraho or Konarak, but with warmth and grace. Some temples are grouped, others isolated, in pleasant settings amid lawns or big trees.

The Orissan landscape between Bhubaneshwar, Konarak and Puri is unspoilt and beautiful; the paddyfields are full of red-wattled lapwings, white egrets and brown paddy-birds. Here and there the road surface is covered with rice, left there by the farmers to be threshed by the traffic or drying out at the verge. The wheels of the Orissan bullock carts are enormous, but thinner in section than any I saw elsewhere; bus and lorry tyres are better for this informal threshing service.

Near Konarak is the big village of Pipli, whose brown mud walls have been intricately decorated with white fingerprint patterns, made by dipping the fingertips into rice flour paste. It looks as if it had been fun to do. But since I first saw Pipli there are more printed posters and less and less finger prints, and what was once a popular art seems to be on the way out.

Dancer, Bhubaneswar

Near Pipli

Lingaraja Temple

Konarak

The great Surya Temple at Konarak stands in an oblong compound surrounded by palms and other trees. This thirteenth-century structure is partly ruined: the lower section, or mandapa, remains, but most of the taller sanctuary, and all of its tower, have vanished. The basement or terrace that supported both of them is intact, with the twelve stone wheels that just enable one to imagine it all as a great chariot. The sides of this terrace are entirely covered – decorated is not the right word – with small carved figures, of elephants and of people, many of them in affectionate or sexual embrace. These seem surprising and maybe even shocking for a moment, until one adjusts to their candour; all are carved with vigour, skill and sharp observation. Their purpose – instruction or celebration – is uncertain. Further up the mandapa, and carved from a harder, shinier stone, are much larger figures of Surya, the Sun god, who gives his name to the temple. Even in its half-broken state, Konarak is a noble and magnificent place.

The visitors inspecting the figures, demure, poker-faced, amused, or slightly stunned, the learned guides explaining them, and pointing out the oddest activities, and the energetic groups climbing up to the higher platforms and terraces, all add movement and interest to the scene. At five-thirty the guardians blow whistles and everyone is unceremoniously herded out through the gates, like circus animals from the ring. Outside the enclosure, coconut sellers wait beside the big green piles of nuts which they pierce open with a couple of expert knife cuts, so that one can drink the milk and scoop out the still half-liquid flesh forming inside. It makes a delicious and refreshing drink.

Surya Temple, Konarak

Konarak

Stone horse and warriors, Konarak

The Stone Horses of Konarak

Four remarkable stone groups stand beside the Surya Temple, two fighting elephants and two horses, each with warriors and victims. One of the elephants is carrying off a defeated warrior in its trunk; the horses are splendidly caparisoned, their harness, saddles and trappings depicted in intricate detail which has survived, clean and sharp, despite damage and weathering. The free-standing isolation of these groups, set well clear of the plethora of sculpture on the temple itself, gives them strength and clarity; the real people around them add beauty.

Konarak stands a mile or so from a beach with a pretty fishing village. South of this the beach stretches away towards Puri. It is undeveloped as yet; there are beautiful little shells on the sand. But one has to watch one's step on the dunes, where I found a recently shed snake skin, delicate and papery.

127

Hotels and fishing boats, Puri

Puri beach

The fishermen's village at Puri consists of a settlement of small houses made of palm leaves, set down just above the high water mark a few hundred yards up from the holidaymakers' part of the beach. The smaller fishing craft lie just below them: sun-bleached timbers formed in beautiful shapes; each boat made in three separate sections, bound together with twine when in the water, but falling apart into the three bits when left on the beach. There are also some much bigger boats, with large fierce glaring eyes painted onto their prows. This strip of beach serves all purposes: the

fascinating business of launching and beaching the boats; the division of the catch – the occasion now and then for some fierce brawling – and the marketing of it by the tough and businesslike fishwives; the drying and mending of delicate nylon nets; and the midday sleep of the exhausted men in the shade beneath their boats.

At the back of the beach are white or candy-coloured concrete villas and hotels, some hard and modern, others – like the beautiful South-Eastern Railway Hotel – with all the trappings of the Raj: Mughal arches and waiters in white uniforms.

128 *Fishing village, Puri*

Fishermen and fishwives, Puri

129

Madras and the South

Southern India is hot, lush, and pretty. Its landscapes are never harsh or overbearing; its pretty hills are planted with tea, coffee, pepper, cloves, cardamom and other exotic spices; its hill stations like Ooty may have seen better days but are surviving as picturesque going concerns, their hotels and palaces full of film people. In the South, the handsome relics left by the Raj are picturesque and endearing rather than oppressive – graceful fortresses, pink-domed law courts in Madras, a long red classical one in Bangalore, some pretty churches, museums and villas. Of course most of it is changing fast – Madras spreading outwards at a great rate, Cochin turned into a major port, tourism transforming places like Kovalam beach whose beauty is too fragile to survive much development unscathed; many of the beautiful teak barges of the Kerala backwaters are dropping out of use.

The South has many monumental temples, of great oddity and beauty. Some are tiny, obscure and isolated; others – as at Madurai – are unbelievably large and complicated, forming a self-contained and vital inner city even within a busy town. The characteristic southern Indian landscape will contain one of several tall temple towers called gopuras or vimanas, painted white or in bright colours, or gilded and gleaming against the sky. There are many elephants in the temples and walking the roads.

I like these places partly for their humming activity, partly for the fascination of the sculpture they contain: not elevated to the sanctified status of artistic treasures but simply left for the time being as part of the working temple scene, free to be used or ignored. The temple rituals and paraphernalia are interesting because although they clearly attract many visitors they do not yet seem artificially created for their benefit: they still seem real and believed in.

Some scenes seemed to me unexpectedly beautiful because of the activity going on there – the long, wide beach at Madras, for example, with its trolleys of orange-coloured fried fish, or the fishermen's beach at Kovalam with its line of piratical-looking fishermen straining at the nets as if at a tug-of-war. One can take a steamy boat trip along the palm-lined canals between Quilon and Alleppey, join the breathless stream of visitors climbing up the rocky hillside at Sravana Belgola to see the big monolithic Jain figure at the top.

There are fewer Mughal buildings in the South, since the Vijayanagar empire long served as a barrier to southward Muslim expansion: the Hindu South is a land not of domed tombs but of tall pyramidal temple gateways like those at Chidambaram [opposite]. And the most spectacular southern palaces are relatively recent, like the Amba Vilas Palace of 1897 at Mysore, designed by Henry Irwin who also built Viceregal Lodge at Shiimla. It looks amazing, especially when outlined and lit up just like Harrods by myriads of electric light bulbs, but not very southern – or indeed Indian.

Southern India feels very different from the north – less developed, gentler and more easy-going, and less affected by civil and sectarian troubles. Its Dravidian people are lovely to look at – darker skinned than northerners, gentler and less aquiline, rounder and softer in the face, and dressed in rich, glowing, intense colours.

Nataraja Temple, Chidambaram

High Court, Madras

Madras

Madras was the earliest of the East India Company settlements in India. This august seniority perhaps contributes to its confident but relaxed and unhurried air: not so busy as Bombay, not so fraught as Calcutta, not so cosmopolitan as Delhi. But it is a big and fast-growing city and it takes a long time to get out of its clutches.

In the richly pink High Court, unusually colourful remnants of Raj splendour and legal elegance can be found around the beautiful, shady courtyards. The skyline is magical, with minarets and onion domes in exotic profusion. The morning scene is delightful as lawyers arrive grandly by car or taxi, put on their legal robes – black silk over sober pinstripe or brilliant saree – and chat and meet clients, or buy legal stationery from the vendors sitting on the ground. These legal activities are familiar and would seem Dickensian were it not for the languorous warmth and the fairy-tale unreality of the skyline. The sea is not far away and one of the tall onion domes serves

also as a lighthouse.

The general air of picturesque legal dignity is slightly offset by the pleasant little huts, made of dried coconut palm leaves, which huddle on the pavement near the grand entrance. Madras has many such reminders of its southern nature, from the tin roofs on some of its churches to the lovely palms which grace its pavements.

The National Art Gallery, by Henry Irwin, is a particularly handsome example of colonial building at its best, using local idioms with skill and imagination. In the Government Museum are fine southern Indian carvings and bronzes: works of extraordinary skill and vivacity. The use of bronze permits not only fine detail but slimness and delicacy of proportion in the figures, quite different from the solidity of stone.

The beach at Madras is lovely. The piles of nets and rope lying about suggest a fishing beach, and at the water's edge there are many barrow boys frying fish dipped in

a bright orange batter. Other barrows are laden with fruit and bananas, seashells, coconuts and soft drinks; there are horses to ride, and plenty of empty sand for them to gallop on. In the late afternoon it feels as though everyone in Madras has come out to the beach to enjoy the scene; the sea cools the air down a little, and it is a relaxed and delightful place; with family groups, trios of women, rings of well-behaved schoolchildren sitting on the sand and playing games, and many bold and self-assured crows.

Fort St George at the northern end of the beach is colonial in the pretty sense: decorative rather than oppressive. St Mary's Church, the oldest Anglican building in the East, was for once too early (1678–80) to model itself on St Martin-in-the-Fields: instead, it might be by Hawksmoor: beautiful, solid and fortress-like. Nearby is a tall flagstaff, and a fine pillared colonial building now serving as the Secretariat.

National Art Gallery

Secretariat, Madras

Church, Madras

Ardanishvara

Marina Beach, Madras

Mamallapuram

Once out of the spreading suburbs of Madras, the coast to the south becomes bare and empty. Sand dunes and widely spaced palms are almost the only features until at length one reaches the small town of Mamallapuram, or Mahabalipuram. This once-modest fishing village is enjoying a heady prosperity as a place of pilgrimage, the shrines being its astonishing rock carvings and its monolithic rock-cut temples. There is fascinating work here: a strange group of half-finished temples or *rathas*, and some carvings of great skill and poetic intensity. One in particular sticks in my mind, of a cow turning to lick its calf: a magical combination of keen observation and warm emotion.

But the most spectacular single building is the Shore Temple, standing virtually on the beach, though now protected by a breakwater of piled-up rocks. The temple has been partly worn away by sea and wind, but is romantically silhouetted and memorable. When I drew it, the morning started breezy and relatively cool; the greyness and the sound of the breakers made me think of Cornwall and Brittany. But soon, lovely coloured figures were walking round the temple; there were several school parties, well-behaved girls in blue shirts, lively teachers under parasols. After wandering round the temple, everyone ends up on the beautiful beach; there are ponies to ride and several girls selling seashells.

Later I was offered a cup of tea in a fisherman's tiny but beautiful house of mud and palm leaves. It seemed to belong to no identifiable period; certainly not to the present. But the present asserts itself clearly enough a few miles down the coast, in the form of a nuclear power station.

Shore temple, Mamallapuram

Thanjavur

Thanjavur and Hindu ceremony

Hindu beliefs and rituals take strange and oddly assorted forms, from the serious and formal temple procession at Srirangam with its parasols and plump policeman, the brilliantly painted roadside shrines, and the gilded temple deities, to the austerely symbolic. The roadside figures are in the care of a fine, thin old priest. They are crudely but vigorously modelled and painted in sharp colours, with staring eyes. The gilded wooden gods and animals in the temples are more skilfully done. The anointed and oily black stone lingams at Thanjavur vividly represent male and female union, but look like machinery in a science museum. There is a long line of these, identically mechanical-looking and inhuman, yet also powerfully suggestive and even sexy.

136

near Maduravantakam

Many of the great southern temples are confusing warrens, only partly open to the sky and seemingly as haphazard in layout as a medieval town; one has only to enter to feel instantly lost. But at Thanjavur all is instantly visible and comprehensible. An entrance way with an elephant at the gate leads to a large oblong courtyard in which stands the great Brihadishwara Temple, quite undiminished by the minor buildings around it. The whole scene has simplicity and majesty; one takes it in and then turns to the surrounding features: the lingams in the side colonnades; the big black stone bull or *Nandi* garlanded under its stone canopy; the documentary film crew laying down a railway for a tracking shot; the visitors scurrying for the shade to avoid burning their bare feet on the scorching paving slabs; and above it all the tall pyramid of the great *vimana* shown here, the clear and obvious climax to the whole complex scene.

Brihadishwara Temple, Thanjavur

Madurai, Tiruchirappalli and Darasuram Temples

At Tiruchirappalli or 'Trichy' the wide and majestic river Cauvery splits into two streams separated by the long and holy island of Srirangam. On this island are two great temple complexes, consisting of concentric walled enclosures with towered gateways, and containing many bazaars and shops as well as various columned halls and inner sanctums. The line of horses opposite form the outermost piers of the Sheshagirirayar Mandapa – they are the outermost part of the structure of this hall, and are not simply decorative additions. The rearing animals are carved with inventiveness and command and with fine detailing of figures and harness; there are friezes of minor figures below. The people who walked past seemed fascinated by these sixteenth-century horses: not just as a routine sight to be noted before passing on, but as something possessing great interest.

At Madurai, the Minakshi Sundareshvara Temple is even more complex and more mystifying, containing many different and seemingly independent enclosures and shrines. Here several of the gopuras or towered gateways were hidden under bamboo scaffolding while being repaired. This was an interesting and, to my surprise, a rather moving place: so much life and fascination and involvement on everyone's part, and so much mystery and oddity in the dark halls where sculptures seem to loom out at one; however sceptical one may feel, it's not a place to make fun of. It was busiest round the Golden Lily tank where this drawing was made; full of high-spirited and energetic visitors wandering about, talking together or sitting and making the place their own, or simply plumped exhausted against the wall. A pretty small bullock cart appeared occasionally [see page 99] and the temple elephant walked past on its way back to its stable at midday.

But in the Airavateshvara Temple at Darasuram, near Thanjavur, no one apart from its own Brahmin priest and an admirable guide appeared all afternoon. This allowed all my attention to focus on the great beauty of the place: the colonnaded courtyard and the temple itself standing in the middle, with a small domed shrine off to one side. Some of the interior columns were carved with astonishing miniature detail: tiny lively figures each the size of matchbox toys. I made this sketch watched by an owl, which now and then gave a loud screech; there were also a few bats, and some squirrels clinging upside down on the sculptures and chirping like birds.

Madurai

Srirangam

Darasuram

Srirangam

Tirumalai Nayaka Palace, Madurai

A Madurai palace and some chariots

The most unexpected building I came
across in the South was also in Madurai,
though not a temple. The Tirumalai
Nayaka Palace of 1636 reminded me
instantly of Pollock's toy theatre scenery –
a courtyard surrounded by plain, colossal
European-looking columns and an exotic
swirl of ogee arches with intricate carving
above them: all in an Indo-Islamic or Indo-
Saracenic style of unimaginable complexity.
There is cool shade in the surrounding
cloisters and in the adjoining throne-room
and hall: all of them enormous, yet still
forming only a portion of the original
palace. The gardeners lent colour and
humanity, and a pleasant touch of
wilderness, to what could easily have been
hard and overbearing.

In the outer courtyard stood a
long-haired and white-bearded holy man,
his forehead covered in white paint: wild
and a bit unprepossessing at first glance,
but friendly and good-natured and
serious-eyed. I felt ashamed of my initial

sense of repulsion. The paraphernalia of
being holy – rags, a staff and an unkempt
look – seem a working uniform to attract
attention.

In many southern India towns there are
one or more big lumbering wooden
chariots, used periodically in temple
processions. They are lovely to look at:
heavy and brutal, yet minutely carved. The
humbler of them, like the one I saw in a tiny
village between Thanjavur and Trichy, are
left out in the open to take their chances
between processions; the grander ones are
pushed into corrugated-iron shelters, like
lock-up garages or kennels, which have a
mysterious fascination in their own right.

Pulling a heavy chariot needs many
people. Even the shrine being carried
round at Shravana Belgola required at least
four pairs of hands. But it takes only one
person to carry a small shrine and a wife to
drum up interest, in order to ward off village
bad luck and pestilence: I saw these people
at Somnathpur.

Somnathpur

Seringapatam

near Tiruchirappalli

Shravana Belgola

Madras

Chidambaram

Kanchipuram

Kumily

Kumily and the Cardamom Hills

The Coromandel coast on the east and the
Malabar coast on the west are separated
by the pretty Cardamom Hills. The village
of Kumily towards their southern end
provides a break in the cross-country
journey. The bus stand and bazaar are at its
centre, very hot at midday – I made this
drawing from the shady doorway of its small
hotel. Nearby is the 'ethnic village' of
Thekkady, with pleasant palm-roofed
houses, gardens with bananas growing in
them, dome-shaped haystacks formed
round upright poles, and black buffaloes in
the fields. There is nothing in fact that
seemed startlingly ethnic, but the place is
quiet and free of traffic and concrete. Big
bats hang thickly, like fruit, from the trees.

On a steep hillside, at the outskirts of
the village is a spice garden: dense
woodland, with bananas, chillis, peppers,
tamarind, coffee, lemon, cocoa, tomato,
and cashew; tapioca and rubber grow
further down towards the plains, and also
an enormous soft-looking fruit, the size of
several pumpkins; tea gardens carpet the
Cardamom Hills with a rich green.

Thekkady

Cardamom Hills

Kovalam

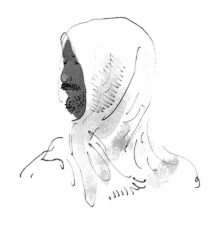

Kovalam was the most southerly point of my journey, not far short of the southern tip of India at Cape Comorin. It has two fine beaches, separated by a rocky point. The smaller southerly beach, backed by rocky hummocks and shaded by groves of palms with cows grazing on the thin turf, is the more sheltered and the more touristy: there is a hotel at each end of it, a few fishing boats, and a curious pink temple at the edge of the sand. Here I drew some nuns in holiday mood, enjoying the sunset after a day out from the Convent of St Anne of Saragoza: friendly, open and conversational.

The northerly beach is wider and longer, curving away to the north as far as one can see. There are many boats. In the morning it is covered with nets and piles of rope and alive with many long lines of fishermen. The process is simple: a boat is launched through the breakers and is rowed out to sea, towing behind it a long rope with a net; it then makes a U-turn and returns to the shore, having left the net to form a loop at the furthest point. Each end of the rope is then pulled energetically in by a line of men, tugging rhythmically as if in a tug-of-war, and singing or chanting in time with the tugging. As the rope shortens and the U-shaped net is itself nearing the beach, eight or nine boys wade waist-high into the shallow water and begin splashing it about to stop the fish escaping round the edge of the net. Finally the net itself is dragged ashore, containing a quivering silver heap of fish, about the size of sardines. Instantly two eager crowds form, one of people, one of crows. The fish are distributed and carried off – most of them in a big basket on someone's head, to be sold. The fishermen each take a few away in small plastic bags. Meanwhile the same process is being repeated by maybe a dozen similar teams further up the beach. Afterwards, towards midday, the piratical-looking, turbaned tug-of-war teams break up and drift away into the palms behind the beach.

Kovalam

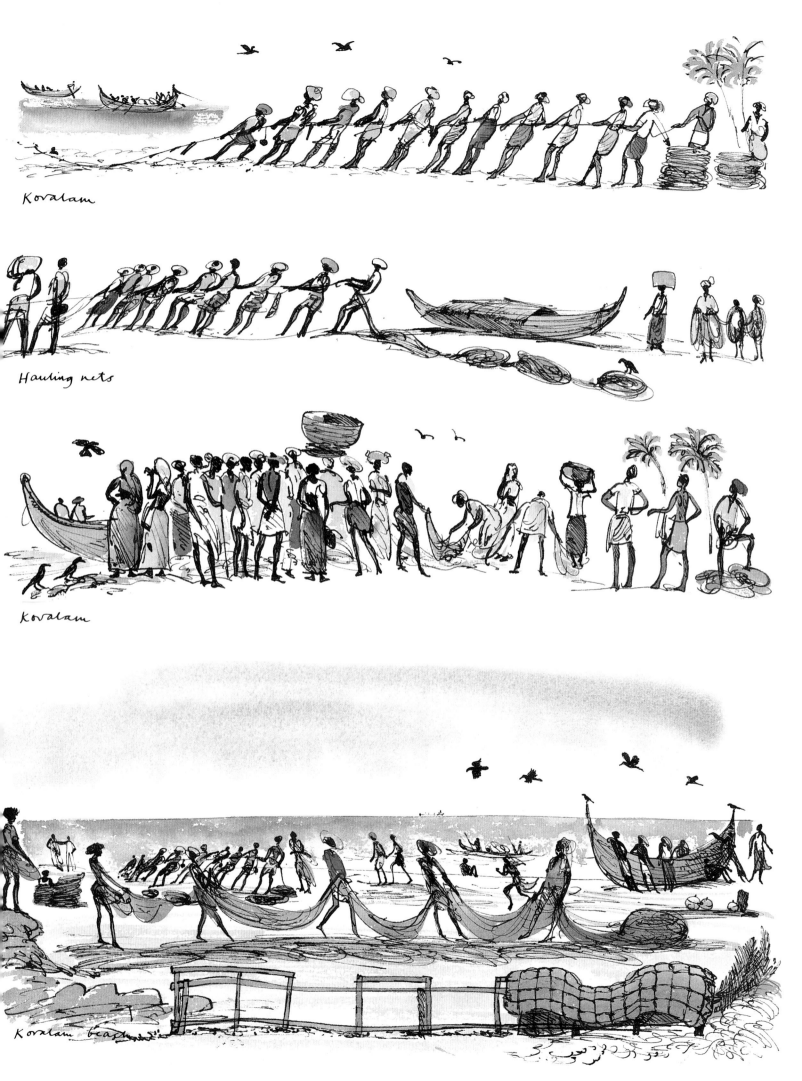

Kovalam

Hauling nets

Kovalam

Kovalam beach

A Nandi, and paddyfields

Nandi in Hindu convention or myth is the bull on which Lord Shiva rides – his mount or 'vehicle'. It is a favourite subject for a carved image. There are many carved Nandis in the South, of all sizes, some of them hewn from enormous monoliths of grey stone. They are usually in the attitude of this one, its further hind leg tucked under the body with the hoof showing through. Nandis are richly decorated with carved chains and bells and their faces have beautiful mild expressions of calm strength, repose and benignity. Hindus respect all animals as fellow beings; this sensible attitude can be sensed in these beautiful and placid Nandi images. Often they are set beside a temple but slightly apart on a plinth in a detached pavilion. This one, on a hill above the city of Mysore, is in the open and unprotected; tended and garlanded by its own priest and surrounded by bold and mischievous

monkeys. Its only other regular companion is the man who sells postcards and feeds sugarcane to the monkeys. They catch the cane in mid air with any of their four hands.

The landscape round Mysore is flat and green, much of the land consisting of paddyfields. These are always lovely, particularly when the rice is young and the flooded fields reflect the sky. To aid irrigation, the fields are subdivided into smaller sections by raised mud dykes or pathways, which are always patrolled by white egrets, or by paddy-birds, a sort of small brown heron. Hidden away in this peaceful and untouched rural countryside is the village of Somnathpur with its beautiful and intricately carved temple. The remarkable thing about the rural southern temples is how peaceful they are; for the present, not many people make the bus or taxi journey out from the city, and one has the place almost to oneself.

Nandi, Mysore

146

paddyfields near Somnathpur

147

Dodda Gaddavahalli

Dodda Gaddavahalli and Shravana Belgola

In the south of Karnataka are many beautiful temples, architecturally complex and intricately carved, and thronged with visitors. On the way to one of these, and slightly off the road, is the small village of Dodda Gaddavahalli, where by the edge of a lake stands a small Lakshmidevi temple of 1113. No one else was there except one or two children from the village, and the only sounds were the cries of water birds from the lake; beyond it rose a landscape of trees and brown hills. I made this drawing from the scorching roof of the gateway into the enclosure; it was a beautiful place. But inside, the temple was dark and quite intimidating; two of the four carved figures were fearful and forbidding, with skeletal bodies and fierce glaring eyes: they were of Bhutanatha and Bhairava, two terrifying aspects of the god Shiva. I felt puzzled by the reverence accorded to these images of divine terror and destruction – maybe as forces to be placated. In Europe, terror and destruction are mostly man-made.

A day or two before, I had visited Shravana Belgola and had climbed the big granite hill of Vindhyagiri to see the Jain temple with the famous image of Gommateshvara at its summit. The steep climb up the 600 steps cut into the granite is exhilarating, as one feels oneself rise above the village and the landscape. The enormous monolithic figure of the saint is smooth and impassive, beautifully carved but slightly inhuman: an idol rather than a person. In the legend, the saint has stood naked in meditation for so long that creepers have twined round his limbs; here he stands woodenly among carved snakes and anthills. Jain figures in general are idealised and rather lifeless, conventionally formalised rather than acutely observed, and always portrayed in the same upright full-frontal stance. They are in consequence boring to look at, however well executed. In darkened Jain temples their jewelled eyes glow out of the gloom, startling but toy-like. Hindu figures have livelier movement, greater vitality, and a stronger curiosity on the sculptors' part.

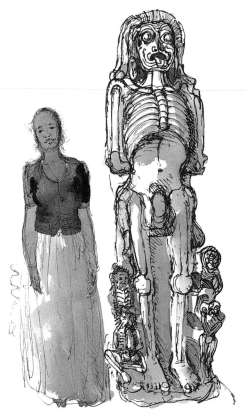

Bhairava

148

Shravana Belgola

149

Ootacamund

Ootacamund nestles high in the Nilghiri Hills, surrounded by a peak or two and by slopes covered with tall eucalyptus trees. It is reached by a spectacular journey on a pretty mountain railway, during which one exchanges the fierce heat of the southern coast for a more temperate climate: waking in Ooty in the cool misty morning one could almost think oneself back in England.

Snooty Ooty was the smartest of all the hill stations; it still has many pretty Raj buildings, even though they are much reduced and run down now. St Stephen's Church (1830) is the most central and the most striking of these; still a going concern, busy with school parties and visitors, with a cow in the churchyard and

a densely wooded hillside of eucalyptus rising behind it. I liked wandering about Ooty, enjoying the tin-roofed and ramshackle Raj remnants, the lake and the Botanical Gardens, Charing Cross, the Library, the Racecourse, the toy train, and Fernhill Palace, the remarkable hotel which used to be the summer palace of the Maharaja of Mysore. This, like my own newer hotel, was full of film people from Bombay shooting a lurid 'hundred-shift' (medium size) gangster production. One of the actors said firmly – and reasonably – that, though it was not an art film of the kind that would be admired in London, it would be very good – something that autorickshaw drivers would like. One

evening during the shooting they all kept breaking off to look at the BBC television news, which seemed a bit slack of them; the *Indian Express* headline next morning was 'Blasts in Bombay kill over 200'.

The place I liked best in Ooty was the bazaar; partly for its beautiful and romantically clothed stall holders and hawkers, and its wild-looking beggars, but also for the craftsmen working on its pavements – shoemakers, cycle repairers, silversmiths with the trays of hot ashes which they heat with a blowpipes in tiny crucibles. The bazaars, the vegetable market and the tongas, the ponies and the cows picking at the rubbish bins, seemed the things least changed in Ooty.

Ootacamund

St Stephen's Church

Alleppey

The Kerala Backwaters

The Kerala Backwaters occupy the low, flat
land that stretches, below sea-level, along
the Malabar coast. It is a hot, wet landscape
in which the small towns of Alleppey and
Quilon are connected with the port of
Cochin by straight palm-shaded canals.
Several kinds of boat ply on the canals –
light skiffs for farm produce, and larger
dugout barges of teak for heavier cargoes
like bricks and copra. These large boats,
with their high Venetian prows and the
hump-backed coverings that protect their
cargoes, look very beautiful, though it's
clearly a hard job for the men who pole
them slowly along. They are now falling
into disuse: too expensive to build, buy
or maintain.

The landscape along the canal banks
looks magical: long perspectives of palm
trees, with some tall betel trees and some

cashews; small farms with thatched roofs
perched on the thin strip of dry land
between canal and paddy; large flocks of
domestic ducks; kingfishers, terns, and a
white-headed kite with a fish in its beak.
My boat chugs along like the *African
Queen*; it is extremely hot; where the canal
widens out and joins another, I have a long
swim, in water that feels hot enough for
a bath. My guide says there have been no
snakes or crocodiles lately; he would rather
talk about Shakespeare, P. B. Shelley, and
Samuel Taylor Coleridge.

At Chungom on the outskirts of Alleppey
the canal banks are lined with long godowns
or warehouses – I make the drawing above
while enjoying the pleasant aroma from a
seed-pressing mill, as small boats piled
high with vegetables and grass for the
cows glide past me.

Near Quilon

152

Cochin

Cochin

Cochin is an ancient and cosmopolitan trading settlement, the oldest in India, which is now fast turning into a big modern port. The river front of the old town still looks as it must have done centuries ago, with Dutch gables, red-tiled godowns and small jetties; there are historic palaces and churches hidden in the streets behind them; the small sailing craft in the harbour are slow, stately and beautiful. But monster tankers berth here too, and at night the sky blazes with lights from dockyard, oil-terminal and container port.

Besides the British, Portuguese and Dutch traders, there was also an ancient Jewish community here, said to date from two centuries BC. Two synagogues still remain. That of the White Jews [opposite] is an enchanting place: a cool, white interior floored with blue tiles from China. It has much polished brass, and lovely clear and coloured glass lamps and chandeliers. But all the younger members of the Jewish community have gone off to Israel and the community is down to sixteen; the

shammes or beadle told me that it would not survive for another generation.

The streets outside it are full of old administrative offices and courts and the bustle of trade – great bundles of coconut fibre being trundled along on trolleys, beautiful low warehouses, long narrow whitewashed streets, a Portuguese palace of 1557 (renovated by the Dutch) with some astonishingly fine Indian frescoes, a bare old Portuguese church (St Francis, c.1546) at the edge of a cricket ground.

Along the water's edge nearby is a line of spectacular Chinese fishing nets. The lacy nets, suspended from a great pivoted arm, are alternately dipped into the water and raised again by four or five men hauling on the counter-weighted timbers at the landward side. It is a picturesque process to watch but laborious to operate; no fish were being caught while I drew. There is a small fish market at the water's edge nearby, but most of its stock must come from the big fleet of fishing boats that docks further up in the harbour.

Cochin

Synagogue, Cochin

Chinese fishing nets, Cochin

High Court, Bangalore

Bangalore

Bangalore is a big sprawling modern capital, whose elegant Raj relics have been happily integrated into a self-confident, spacious and prosperous new city. This integration is at its most dramatic in Cubbon Park, where two colossal administrative buildings, one from the Raj, one from the present day, face each other across pleasantly laid out gardens. The High Court is classical, of red stucco, with a central Ionic portico and immensely long arcaded wings to either side; these terminate in smaller, plainer porticos, which echo but do not compete with the central pedimented one. Right opposite the High Court, and standing on higher ground which allows it comfortably to upstage everything else, is the imposing Vidhana Soudha, comprising the Secretariat and the State Legislature. On this white granite edifice Indian features – domes, chatris – adorn and dignify what is essentially a monster office block, just as in London Lutyens used classical features to face his City offices. The road that separates the two long buildings is essentially Indian, with fruit barrows, cold-drinks stalls, horse buggies and red and white double-decker buses. In the gardens, stiffish statues of Indian heroes like Nehru look down on groups of gardening women, patiently swishing away at the grass with twig brooms and filling big sacks with dried leaves.

There is plenty more in Cubbon Park to remind one of the old order and the new. It is a pleasant place with plenty of big trees and a line of shady benches where several courting couples were holding hands – not altogether unlike the Luxembourg Gardens, apart from the thickets of bamboo and the coconut sellers. There are excellent statues of Queen Victoria and of King Edward VII in hot-looking and highly unsuitable robes; the francophile prince

158

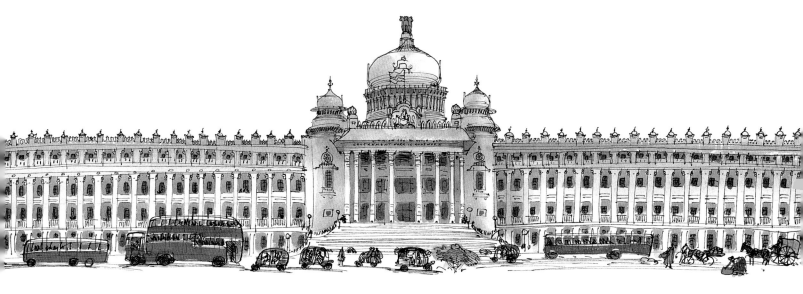

Vidhana Soudha, Bangalore

lends a French touch to these pleasant
gardens, and there is a very un-Indian
Great War memorial – a soldier from the
trenches, looking extremely out of place
here; no Indian names survive on its plaque.
There is a red church which matches the
High Court, and a tough-looking old
railway engine outside the Technology
Museum, alongside the first Indian jet
fighter – Bangalore has an aircraft industry.
This jet of course looks international:
there is nothing to tell one in what
continent it originated. It is the first thing
in this book, apart from the Howrah
Bridge, of which this could be said.

   The same could not be said of the
brilliantly coloured and rather crudely
executed mythical figures arranged round
a small grotto in the beautiful Lalbagh
Botanical Gardens. It is this vigorous
survival of the Indian past into the
technological present that seems so strange
to a visitor to India. It is easy to warm to
images of the traditional deities when their
figures have been softened, given mysterious
imprecision, transformed into 'art' by the
passage of time; it is harder when, as here,
they seem popular, sharp, colourful and
vulgar. In a corner of the gardens is a tiny
zoo, where a crocodile lies, hot, lazy and
fed-up: motionless all morning apart from
an occasional widening of one eye. These
gardens are well laid out, with fine mature
trees and dense thickets of tropical growth
– more like 'the jungle' as I'd imagined it
as a child than anything else I saw in India.
Outside the gardens, red double-decker
buses run along fine straight roads as if
jungles were in another continent entirely;
posters stuck on the trees are for lectures on
Karl Marx and Stalin. There is a cottage
containing the Animal Protection Society,
and a beautiful Government Museum,
with a fine interior but short on labels.

Pavement and Jungle

I drew these pavement fruit and vegetable stalls in various southern towns: Ooty, Hyderabad, Bangalore. The traders, though often rough-looking, were always friendly and assured, and expert at relating with other people, in which they have had plenty of practice; their customers were shyer, intent on their purchases and anxious not to make a bad buy. I like watching such exchanges: no image, no presentation, no added value, no hype and no hard sell, just the simple trade in real commodities – melons, limes, oranges, grapes, sweetcorn – that people need and want.

But of course, besides these good things, people also want and need a bit of fun, a touch of romance. Hype and hard sell are always to hand on the film posters on the hoardings: often cut-outs expertly painted by hand on big rickety-looking structures held up by bamboo poles. The actor's painted image here is itself garlanded with long ropey swathes of real flowers.

The pavements are not a bad workplace for these fruit sellers. There is plenty of life to enjoy or to watch; you can feed your baby or lie down and have a sleep; people are glad to see you, and appear to respect you; you are not shut away in an office, frustrated or bored; you are unlikely to lose your job.

Hyderabad

Ootacamund

Tiruchirappalli

Bangalore

Lalbagh Gardens, Bangalore

Gol Gumbaz, Bijapur

Karnataka and Goa

This is a region of beautiful and undeveloped landscapes; of gentle and intensively cultivated plains, rock-strewn hills and green mountains, and of small towns, whose streets are still full of cows and donkeys, buffaloes, goats, kids, pigs and piglets, dogs, watercarts, children, tongas and bikes each with three or four riders. Here are found the rich and fascinating remnants of earlier civilisations, ancient and Hindu (especially at Badami, Aihole, and Vijayanagara) and Muslim (at Bijapur). At Goa are the pretty but extremely alien monuments – cathedrals, churches, cannons – of colonialism in its conquering Portuguese form, in which great sacred and monastic structures are huddled together like fortresses in hostile territory, while the towers of smaller isolated churches stick up from the paddyfields like fingers of icing-sugar – or like the tall red and white radio masts that keep the country in touch today. Here in Karnataka are caves, temples, palaces, churches – easily differentiated and very distinct buildings: all of individuality and, in their different ways, perfection.

All these places are survivors from much grander and more powerful pasts. Bijapur is an astonishing place to look at, but stripped of its fine monuments it would be no more than a modest, spread-out village: it is hard now to imagine it as a great fortress capital, even if its mosques and palaces still remain there as proof. The mighty and famous Golgumbaz [opposite] still stands to testify to the Indian genius for building, enclosing a larger unbroken space under a single dome than any other building in the world. In Bijapur it is the buildings that are remarkable: the surrounding landscape is flat and a bit dull. But in Badami the caves and temples cannot be imagined separately from the landscape. This is of romantically towering rock formations around a lake or tank; the most interesting man-made structures, the cave temples, are cut straight into the rock, their wonderful sculpture as much part of the natural hillside as are the columns and terraces and the swirling formations of the rock itself.

At Hampi or Vijayanagara, although the architecture is built rather than hollowed out, the beauty of the rocky landscape and the extreme interest of the temples and palaces are again inseparable. Here too the landscape permeates the site: swaying groves of coconut palms and bananas surrounding the stone and brick temples, the beautiful river Tungabhadra flowing past and enhancing the sacred centre, the boulder-strewn hills providing both building material and backdrop. Vijayanagara's importance during its powerful heyday from the fourteenth to the sixteenth centuries was as the great Hindu capital which kept at bay the Muslim and Persian influences so dominant at Bijapur, and stopped them penetrating further into southern India – major Muslim buildings stop at Bijapur.

After Vijayanagara's mystery and isolation, arriving in Goa is a surprise. With its pungent colonial echoes, its convents, cathedrals and churches, cloisters and cannons, it is for a European a step back into a more familiar – if not more congenial – world. Goa is a delightful place with its shimmering paddy fields, its palm-fringed beaches and its tin-roofed Courts of Justice. But as far as architecture goes, it seems halfway home.

Bhutanatha group temples, Badami

Badami and Bijapur

As one approaches Badami, the flattish
fields of cotton, cane, millet and ground
nuts give way to rocky sandstone outcrops,
with great hunks of rock as big as hills
rearing dark and dramatic against the sky.
Along this distant skyline appear tiny insect-
like lines of figures carrying loads of
firewood on their backs. Cradled and
almost encircled within this ring of rock is
an artificial lake, with the big village of
Badami at one end and a cluster of temples,
the Bhutanatha group, at the other. In
between, steps lead down to the water and
women do the laundry in it as their
children play around them. Ripples in the
middle of the lake show that snakes,
'small but dangerous', are swimming there.
On one of the hilltops there are fortifications
and temples; cut into the opposite hillside
are four remarkable temples, dark and
impressive, many of their walls and ceilings
covered with extremely beautiful sculpture
[see overleaf]. The sculptures tell stories or
point morals: a donkey's head on a
woman's body suggests that love is blind.
The subject matter includes every

creature that people would have been
familiar with: cows, bulls, cobras, eagles,
fish, crocodiles; it is as though life itself
had taken root on these walls. On the
terraces outside them, groups of monkeys
roam and gibber and help themselves to any
oranges rashly left unattended in sketching
bags.

The curious rocks above the caves are
seen opposite at the top right; the smaller
but dramatically piled-up boulders are at
Kodakali on the way to Hampi. The
drawings beneath them are of some of the
fine arches in Bijapur, mostly ruined but
impressive and poignant at the same time
and reminding one, despite the mud and the
emptiness, of how splendid Bijapur must
once have been.

In the watercolour of Badami [overleaf],
the lake appears centrally with the square
school enclosure near it. The drawing was
made just inside the third cave temple, of
c.578. It was raining intermittently; as the
light came and went, the figures grew more
indistinct until I could half imagine them
watching me in the gloom.

Kodakali

Badami

Bijapur

Bijapur

Bijapur

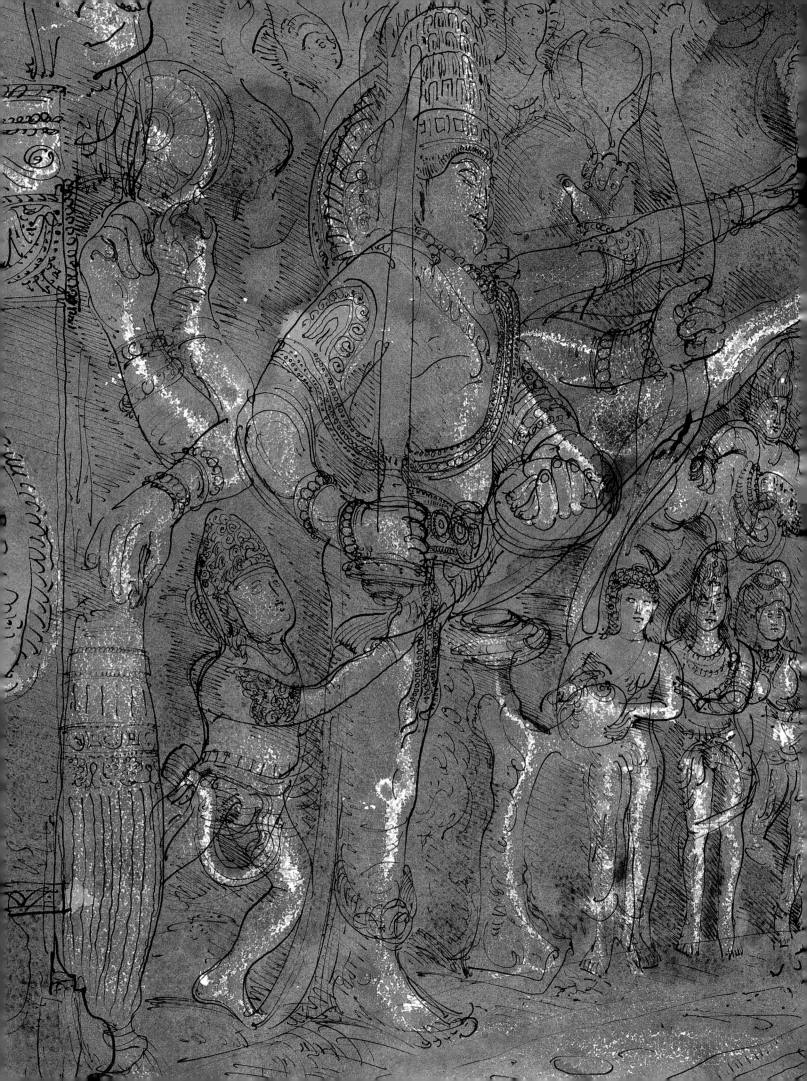

Cave 3, Badami

Vijayanagara or Hampi

At Vijayanagara or Hampi, the extremely pretty countryside and the wonderful ruins complement and enhance each other. The drawing above was made from the slopes of Matanga Hill, looking towards the gopura or entrance tower of the Virupaksha Temple, which recalls the many other fine gopuras of southern India. The long straight colonnaded street stretching away towards it was once lined with houses; their bare stone skeletons, one- or two-storeyed, empty but solidly built, remain at each side. Nearer the temple they have acquired a new life as shops and cafés. Behind them are fields of bananas and palms; as I drew, cattle and buffaloes wandered or were driven by herdswomen up the hill past my shaded vantage point.

A large river, the Tungabhadra, flows nearby. On its banks, a mile or so away, stands the Vitthala Temple, in whose courtyard is a splendid stone chariot. Vijayanagara spreads widely over the countryside, but it has two main centres. The chariot and the temple above are both within the Sacred Centre. To its south, away from the river, is the Royal Centre, where the watchtower drawing was made; it shows the battered (i.e. inwardly sloping) protecting wall round the Lotus Temple. Just outside it stand the Royal Elephant stables, eleven domed chambers in a long straight row; an extremely grand building, with a lovely skyline, but no longer occupied by elephants. The white bullocks on the lawn were being minded by a woman who also sold coconuts; in a long hot afternoon I was her only customer.

The drawing overleaf is from the steep northern side of Matanga Hill, its boulders overlooking the sixteenth-century Tiruvengalanatha temples. In their present state, it is easy to see the characteristic division of such buildings, the lower parts of stone and the upper brown brick, which would have been plastered; and also the division of the temple enclosure into inner and outer walled areas. To its left extends the long green perspective of the Sule Bazaar, another colonnaded chariot street, running towards the river. I made this drawing in the shade of a boulder the size of a house. Sections of other boulders have been drilled and split off for building blocks, but not used. It was a pleasant place to draw – I can't remember one more beautiful. There were a few people climbing past, and cattle, monkeys, lizards, eagles, parrots and doves, large butterflies and a brown caterpillar some ten inches long. No snakes were visible, but the grass rustled behind me. Vijayanagara is the place I would most like to go back to.

Stone chariot

Watchtower

Elephant stables

Tiruvengalanatha temple, Vijayanagara

Goa – a Panaji church

Goa is a beautiful and romantic place, of beaches and palms, rice-fields and tropical rivers; still indelibly permeated by the works of the orderly but fierce Portuguese, who only left in 1961. Their neat and prettily coloured houses, their fine legal and administrative buildings, and their churches and convents are Goa's distinctive architectural features. The original settlement was at Old Goa, a few miles up one of the rivers that penetrate the colony; here the Portuguese built an overwhelming concentration of enormous churches, a cathedral, basilica, convents and chapels and a Palace of the Inquisition (luckily now vanished) all within a few hundred yards of one another. The remaining churches, however spectacular or pretty, still seem a bit excessive, a disproportionate invasion. Old Goa is now only a village; once fever-ridden and a prey to epidemics, it was abandoned in favour of Panjim or Panaji, nearer the mouth of the river. Here, at the head of a fine symmetrical staircase, stands one of the prettiest churches, of the Immaculate Conception, in Portuguese Baroque style.

I drew outside it as evening mass went on within: the music (harmonium and violins) that drifted out was a pretty blend of Indian and European, the congregation as docile and contented as my daughters once seemed as snowflakes in their school nativity play. Mass was preceded and followed by fanfares and drumming by a bugler and a blind drummer on the steps outside; they also set off big thunderflashes at the raising of the host. The drawing below is of one of the many beautiful older houses in and around Panaji, many of which now look neglected and shabby.

But other handsome official buildings, like the High Court, are well maintained; and the riverside situation gives the place great beauty, even if at low tide it smells tropical and a little dangerous. Many smaller houses not unlike the one below have been built among the coconut groves that back the magnificent beaches, widely enough spaced out to retain great charm. But Goa is now vulnerable, subject to a new invasion of jumbo jetloads of charter-flight visitors. How long can it hope to absorb them and still retain its rich individuality?

Panaji

Church of the Immaculate Conception, Panaji

cloister, Bom Jesus, Old Goa

Baroque Churches of Old Goa

The enormous Basilica of Bom Jesus in Old Goa is built of brown laterite, which distinguishes it from the other white-painted churches. It contains a great shrine, the chapel and tomb of St Francis Xavier. Large crowds were queueing up under the palms to see it, and the cloisters of the Basilica were full of families of visitors camping out, getting dressed and making breakfast on primus stoves – a curious-looking and good-natured bunch, hard to place, with mingled Indian and European aspects in dress and physical appearance.

Some foundations and the ruins of a tall tower are all that remains of the nearby Church of St Augustine, a jagged and insecure-looking finger pointing upwards above the palms and mangroves. Lines of women were at work round it, carrying flat baskets of sand and cement on their heads. Beyond it is the Convent of St Monica.

The Church of St Francis of Assisi stands at the edge of a grassy and palm-fringed Campo Santo opposite the Basilica. This open space was thick with nuns and with lay-sisters carrying loads of cathedral chairs on their heads. Some beggars were resting their crutches on the pavement; worn-out people, exhausted by visiting the three big churches and the convent museum were drinking orange frootis and straw-drink mango juice at the pleasant, shady café. Behind the church and nearer the river is the grand Italianate façade of the Church of St Cajetan.

The other two churches opposite are more rural; one faces Panaji from a line of mangroves across the river, the other stands at the edge of rice-fields on the way to Calangute Beach, once famous for its hippies. None were about when I was there, though I did see a few G-strings. This beach is most beautiful: an apparently endless expanse of clean firm sand, separated from the small coastal road by groves of palms keeping the new beach hotels pretty well out of sight.

174

St Augustine, Old Goa

St Cajetan, Old Goa

near Panaji

St Francis, Old Goa

near Pilar

175

Goa – palms and people

Every scene in Goa is softened and made
graceful by the presence of tall feathery
palms: framing the distant tankers and
container ships in the harbour; providing a
long shady tunnel between gleaming
paddyfields and a backdrop for their
monotonous flatness; enfolding the white
churches and the red-tiled convents;
engulfing the swampy riverside houses
between Old Goa and Panaji; helping to
screen the beaches from encroaching
development; and turning the baroque
pomposity of the Portuguese colonists into
harmless theatrical jungle.

To harvest them and keep them in good
shape, the coconut palms need the attention
of a professional climber. He climbs with
the help of two coils of twine wound
round the trunk, one for his feet, one for
a hand-hold; having shooed everyone away
from the ground far below, he prunes the
dead leaves and cuts down the coconuts with
a sharp steel machete. He was a friendly
and self-reliant man; he must also have been
careful and methodical, to have survived at
all. He was working in the coconut groves
behind Calangute Beach, a long expanse of
sand, and very hot; the women were
working nearby, collecting firewood and
selling fruit to the few tourists on the beach.

Calangute Beach, Goa

Panaji

near Mapusa

near Panaji

Convent, Old Goa

Mandovi River

Calangute Beach

near Panaji

Viceroy's Arch, Old Goa

Bombay

Bombay is extraordinary: a great tropical seaport city, in parts brand-new, shiny and successful, in other parts unbelievably mean and degraded. It is a place of wealth and squalor, without visible safety nets: a city of true Victorian values. So it is fitting that it should possess a spectacular and unrivalled quantity of Victorian buildings, familiar enough in style to make the jet-lagged Londoner feel half at home, yet looking exotic and strange because of the tropical vegetation, the brown dried grass of the maidans, and the hurrying, hard-pressed, shirt-sleeved or sareed crowds of business people.

The Victorian architecture is there because British Bombay was not primarily a military or administrative capital, a Raj cornerstone like Calcutta and Delhi, but an astonishingly prosperous commercial city, with law courts, fine schools and a university, and connected with the rest of the subcontinent by its vast and beautiful railway stations. It is true that later on Bombay also became a rhetorical point of entry for the final generation or two of imperialists who stepped ashore at the Gateway of India (1927) and put up at the old and magnificent Taj Hotel just behind it – two notable high-intensity experiences. But by then the old order was on its last legs; and the Gateway, however convincingly Indian it looks, was a British pastiche, a stage set – not for real. The law courts and the university and the great stations *are* real; as real as the huddled shanty-town roofs you fly over as the plane lands.

Until recently the city's magnificent and picturesque skyline, its domes and spires and gothic pinnacles, rose unchallenged. Now of course they have to take their chance, as everywhere, in the free-for-all of new high-rise commercial building. But from close up they look unharmed and as beautiful as ever.

Bombay has its extremes. I drew from the splendid old Taj, whose windows have one of India's great views. But through the kindness of a Bombay doctor who had worked in the fishermen's village near the airport, I was also able to draw in one of the village's tiny one-room houses, occupied now by an autorickshaw driver and his family. This too had a sort of beauty. Later, a taxi driver showed me a few of the grander sights and then, unprompted, took me to see some of the more lurid – not just the extraordinary laundry, but the Falkland Road red-light district, where I drew until chased away, and a nightmarish street where people lived sheltered only by tarpaulins held down by old car tyres. Here I naturally felt a voyeur. But such places are as much the legacy of empire as the splendid railway stations and the fine university: one can't feel half-proud of the one but uninvolved in the other.

Bombay also has its easily overlooked minor delights – the piles of coconuts, fruit and roasted sweetcorn sold from the pavements; the old double-decker buses; the beautiful curve of Marine Drive reaching round from Nariman Point to Malabar Point; the pools of water lying on the cricket pitch in front of the Gymkhana Club; the bullock carts carrying big blocks of ice; the energy and vivid beauty of the men and women on the streets. Some of them are perhaps a bit more 'western' in manner than in other Indian cities, but only superficially so, as the dusty pavement shrines and the women digging up the roads bear witness.

Rajabai clocktower, Bombay

179

The Taj and the Gateway

The Taj Hotel was built in 1903 by the architect Chambers. It is an impressive and lovely building, in a remarkable setting: with a pretty skyline of coloured domes and towers, and delicate detailing of the white woodwork within its big, bold silhouette. The tall new Taj extension next door does it little credit, though from its high-level restaurant there is a fine view down onto the Gateway of India; but I still prefer the famous first-floor outlook from the old Taj's Sea Lounge, onto the promenade with its horse-drawn coaches and its eel catchers, and onto the coloured boats, tied up or making the hour-long harbour trip. It's from these boats that one gets the best view of the Gateway and the Taj together, changing their relative scale: the looming Gateway seeming to shrink and the Taj to rise as the boat pulls away from the steps.

The Gateway, timelessly Indian though it now seems, was actually built twenty-four years after the Taj. After another twenty-four India was independent. I had enjoyed wandering among the crowds beneath and around it on my first visit to India, and drinking in the heady sense of being in the East. It commemorates the royal visit of 1911 and it is both touching and slightly ridiculous, like many earnest monumental memorials. It looks more indestructible than the old Taj but not nearly so pretty.

Taj Hotel and Gateway of India

Azad Maidan, Bombay

Cricket, working and living in Bombay

Three open spaces or maidans keep the centre of Bombay green, or at least tawny – Oval Maidan in front of the university, Cross Maidan, and Azad Maidan near Victoria Terminus. These greens are enlivened by much cricket, watched from the edge of the pitch with the same slightly wistful attentiveness as in England. Cricket is played everywhere in India, on grass or mud, at dusty urchin level or in front of grand and comfortable clubs. Here on Azad Maidan the outfield serves for drying sarees on.

Churchgate Station is at the corner of Oval Maidan; rush hour in the morning is spectacular, with tightly packed trains shuttling in and out and others pulling in almost before the platform clears. It looks like a vision of decent conformity, of hard

work that has become second nature and accepted as one's lot.

I was taken into the fishermen's village off the airport road by a friend who had been the village doctor, and who was welcomed warmly by the people there. I came along with some misgivings, but they were unnecessary. We went into several houses: some now done-up and grand; others, like the one opposite, tiny – I have made it look much bigger than it really was. This single room is the home of the five people in it: the husband Vijay, who drives an autorickshaw; his wife Nisha; their young child and their baby; and a granny. The room serves as kitchen, living-room and bedroom for them all; there is a small separate bedroom in the tiny attic under the roof, reached by ladder. Inside this and the

other houses, everything was very clean and well kept, with shiny kitchen utensils and clean clothes; there was great courtesy and friendliness. Outside, open drains at the edge of the road carry away household water, as in any Indian village: it seemed simple and efficient and smelt fresh. There is no sanitation in the village: people just go to the beach.

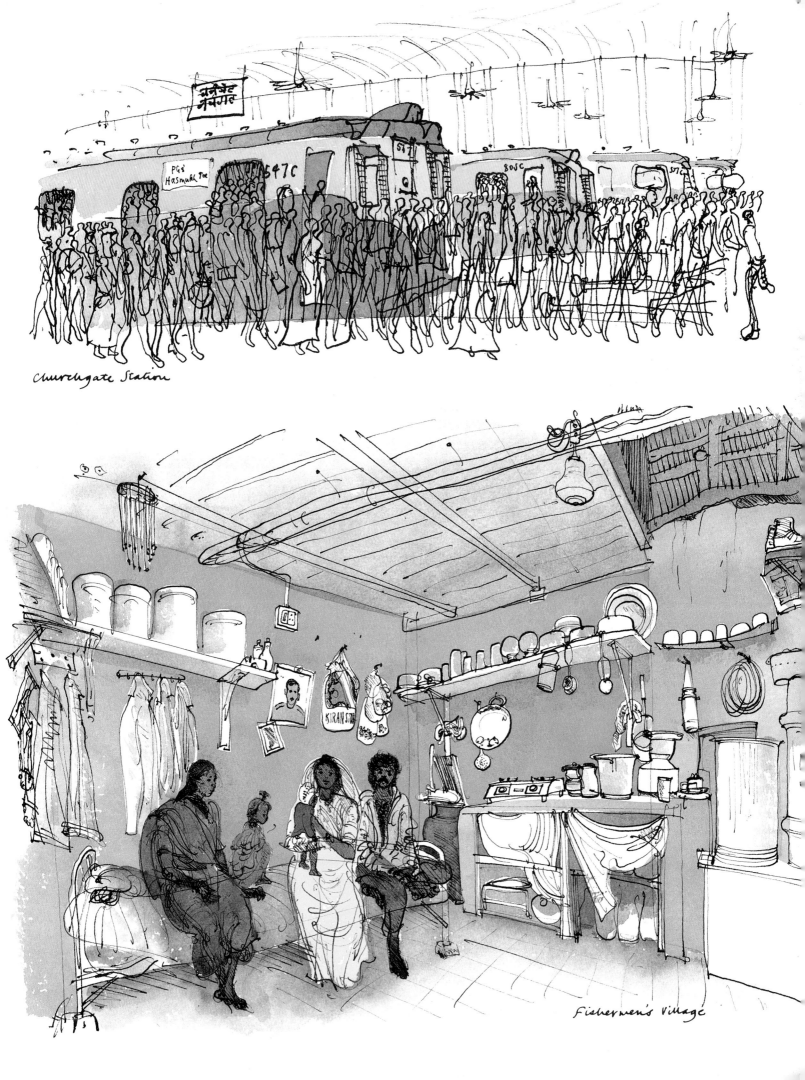

Churchgate Station

Fishermen's Village

Pavement, Bombay

Bombay's pavement life and an open-air laundry

It was in this street that Bombay existence seemed at its most shocking. It was not just the fact of living on the pavement, but the dreary hugger-mugger of the ramshackle roofs and the rubbish and old tyres that held the plastic sheeting in place, and the din of the traffic only a yard or two away from the string beds. It all looked spectacularly awful. And yet the life that was going on here, though cramped and public, did not seem utterly degraded; rather, it looked adaptable, co-operative and friendly, or as much so as family life does anywhere else: people resting or sleeping, mothers doing their daughters' hair, chatting, taking the baby for a walk. India often shocks one into making instant and superior judgements, and then as quickly it forces one to think again. No outsider can

truly say what kind of life is acceptable for someone else; and in any case one has no power to influence it. One can only look and remember things as they are.

A Bombay taxi driver took me, unasked and more or less as a matter of course, to see some unexpectedly bizarre oddities: one of the municipal crematoria, the red-light district, and this highly organised laundry. Here the mystery of what happens to dirty clothes between breakfast and dinnertime the same evening was cleared up a bit. Some at least go off to this well-organised centre, of white concrete and grey-green running water, behind the railway line: there to be washed laboriously in the open air by male hands and pressed by female ones, out of sight beneath the awnings and canopies. In this scene of unremitting hard work there

are hardly any concessions to mechanised productivity: the dirt is beaten out by hand. Labour is still more plentiful than machinery: there are more hands than jobs.

The whole of the laundry is sunk below street level. I made this drawing at mid-morning from the pavement, from a sort of impromptu viewing platform where other tourists with cameras and videos would also stop to look, be briefly amazed, and pass on, a reaction the Bombay people took for granted. In the distance is Bombay's other, more unfamiliar skyline – not the elegant Victorian one of grand European university buildings and fine railway stations, but a Douanier Rousseau prospect of palms and distant factory chimneys sweltering in the tropical heat; kites and airliners turn lazily in the sky.

Nautch girls, Bombay

Laundry, Bombay

185

The Victoria Terminus

The Victoria Terminus of 1878–87 is still the most extraordinary building in Bombay: monumental and noble in its conception, fascinating in its decorative and sculptural detail, its exotic tropical setting emphasised by the tall palms in front of it, its original purpose still fulfilled hourly as thousands flood in and out of the city through its arches. The Victoria Terminus is a great and useful place. The teeming street in front of it is also endlessly fascinating; the busy shopkeepers and traders around me as I drew were accommodating and helpful.

The tall Municipal Buildings of 1893 on the left look as if they could almost be part of the station, and are indeed the work of the same architect, F. W. Stevens: a European, but working brilliantly in an Indian context, as the Raj itself must have seemed for a while to be doing in the aftermath of the Mutiny. These two buildings are practical and useful, not empty and rhetorical: true monuments, worthwhile things to have left behind.

Victoria Terminus, Bombay

187

Bombay – Churchgate Street and Marine Drive

Churchgate Street, Bombay

Bombay's beauty lies in its mixtures, its contrasts: of planned and accidental, tidy and scruffy, old and new. These contrasts are vivid in the morning on the crowded pavement opposite Churchgate Station, as traders set up stalls and the shops too spread out onto the pavement, while the rush hour fills the street and morning commuters surge out from the station. The battered old red buses and the domed towers across the road belong to the older Bombay, as do the laden people; but even in this scene new high-rise concrete and pylons have appeared.

They are thicker on the ground along Marine Drive [opposite], where substantial thirties buildings are now dwarfed by big international-looking offices and hotels, and from where one can look across Back Bay to a hazy Malabar Hill gleaming with an almost unbroken row of white towers. These tall buildings are smart and new, and good of their kind, though they could of course be anywhere in the world. There have been a few snags in this eager transition from older to newer: the interior of the Air India building on the left had recently been

wrecked by a bomb. Few venture down onto the smelly black rocks piled below, and no one now swims in the water. But Marine Drive always looks beautiful: especially later in the day when people come to enjoy the cool breeze from the sea and the waving palms, to sit on the wall and wander along past the beggars and the sweetcorn and coconut stalls and the men selling cold drinks. These things are old, familiar, and Indian; and this was the last drawing I made there, before catching the midnight plane back to London.

Marine Drive, Bombay

'These people must have been so very magnificent in what
they did before we Europeans came here with our bad money-
making ways. We have made it impossible for them to do
more, and have let all they accomplished go to ruin.'
FANNY EDEN, *Indian Journals*, 1837–8

Index